Graffiti in the Ivy League

Other Books In This Series:

GRAFFITI
IN THE
IVY LEAGUE
(and thereabouts)

Marina N. Haan
Richard B. Hammerstrom

WARNER BOOKS

A Warner Communications Company

Copyright © 1981
by Brown House Galleries, Ltd.

Warner Books, Inc.,
75 Rockefeller Plaza,
New York, N. Y. 10019

A Warner Communications Company

Cover design by Gene Light

Cover art by Jack Davis

Artistic enhancement by Jerry Mymudes,
Marina Haan, and Richard Hammerstrom

First printing: September 1981

10 9 8 7 6 5 4 3 2 1

Printed in the United States of America

Library of Congress Cataloging in Publication Data

Haan, Marina N.
    Graffiti in the ivy league (and thereabouts)

    1. Graffiti—Northeastern States.   2. College
students—Northeastern States—Attitudes.   3. Ivy
League (Football conference)   I. Hammerstrom,
Richard B.   II. Title.
GT3913.N94H3   081   81–2867
ISBN 0–446–37003–7 (U.S.A.)   AACR2
ISBN 0–446–37082–7 (Canada)

DEDICATION

*This book is dedicated to the twentieth-century
architects who replaced stone in the stalls of the Ivy
League with other materials that are easier to write
on, thus making our work possible.*

AUTHORS' NOTE

The Northeast—mecca of the arts, center of fashion, leader of commerce, bank of the world, reservoir of power.

What is it that sets the Northeast apart as the leader in so many areas? Is it the mere accident of geography? We think not. Is it the lingering of historical experience? Again, we think not.

The continuing impact of the Northeast on American life cannot be so easily explained. The answer lies deeper.

The strength of the Northeast lies in its people. In particular, in those who lift themselves to success, lift themselves to the stages, the boardrooms, and the executive offices of the Northeast. They are what makes the difference.

And how do these people come about the characteristics that lead to success? That's the question we asked ourselves.

There may be many factors, but one seems obvious: the educational experience of the Northeast. It is in the centers of higher education that the drive for achievement is developed. It is there that students are prepared for the challenging world that will face them. And, logically, it was there, in the colleges of the Northeast, that we decided to go to find the secrets of success.

We determined early on not to use surveys or interviews. Surveys tend to be misguided. Interviews tend to be self-serving. We wanted a reliable source of data on students in the Northeast.

In the end we decided to use the most basic source of information, what the students wrote for themselves—graffiti. We would find the secret to success on the walls of the Northeastern colleges!

There was no question of where to start our inquiries. We would go first to the Ivy League schools. These bastions of tradition and achievement would undoubtedly provide many of the answers that we sought.

Beyond the Ivy League, we would go to other institutions of the Northeast where there was either a great level of success among graduates or a great number of students who would be writing on the walls.

The plan was carried out. We went to the schools. We gathered the graffiti. We made our discoveries.

On the pages that follow we present our data. From this information you may well find the secret to success. If not that, you may at least find some enjoyment.

Marina N. Haan
Richard B. Hammerstrom

CONTENTS

Graffiti in the Ivy League

U of Rhode Island – Kelly Hall

Northeastern scholastic institutions themselves play a significant role in the achievements of their graduates. Students are not reluctant to express their appreciation and affection.

THERE ARE NO WOMEN AT DARTMOUTH, ONLY MEN WHO HAVE WORKED THEIR BALLS OFF.

DARTMOUTH – WILDER HALL

Nuke Cambridge!

Dartmouth – Wilder Hall

HARVARD—LOVE IT!

HARVARD – WIDENER LIBRARY

HARVARD IS FULL OF STUPID TEACHERS AND STUDENTS!
HARVARD – BIOLOGICAL LABS

A liberal arts degree from Harvard ain't worth shit!
Harvard – Widener Library

THE LOGICAL PROGRESSION OF MY CAREER AT
HARVARD:
FIRST I WORKED MY ASS OFF.
THEN I FOUND OUT IT DIDN'T SIT RIGHT.
NOW I DON'T GIVE A SHIT.
HARVARD – BIOLOGICAL LABS

Why is Harvard so great?
—no sex to distract from studies

—below—

—because it says it is

—below—

—because it is

—below—

—who says it is? I like Yale.
Harvard – Jefferson Hall

HARVARD RULES!

YALE – DUNHAM LAB

YALE SUCKS!

HARVARD – PIERCE

(beside picture of penis)
Portrait of a typical Yale professor.

Yale – Law

NOTICE: THE SENIOR FACULTY IS INVITED TO AN ALTERNATIVE CAREERS MEETING IN ROOM 217.

YALE – GRADUATE SCHOOL

I wonder if Jerry Ford ever chewed gum here?

Yale – Graduate School

HAS ANYONE SEEN NEW HAVEN? PLEASE RETURN IT TO THE LOST AND FOUND.

YALE – LAW

HERE I SIT BROKEN-HEARTED.
CAME TO PENN AND BECAME RETARDED.

PENN – DIETRICH LIBRARY

Penn Liberation! Wipe out student activism! Apathy can destroy Penn in your lifetime!

Penn – Williams Hall

4

PENN—NO THANKS!

PENN – RITTENBERG LAB

Sadly, the intelligence climate at Penn is so dry that little we do is likely to threaten the misfit exploitation system enough to provoke any response.

–below–

But I'm gonna raise Hell anyway.

Penn – Williams Hall

WHARTON IS OVERRATED AS HELL.

– BELOW –

U OF PENN IS OVERRATED TOO.

– BELOW –

WE ARE ALL A BUNCH OF HARVARD, PRINCETON, YALE, BROWN, AND STANFORD REJECTS.

PENN – WHARTON SCHOOL OF FINANCE & COMMERCE

VISIONS OF UNCERTAINTY,
REBELLIOUS MEDIOCRITY,
SET SUPERIORITY,
THAT'S WHAT PRINCETON MEANS TO ME.

PRINCETON – ARCHITECTURE

Is Princeton bio-degradable?

Princeton – Guyot Hall

WHY DON'T WE GO, YOU AND I, WHILE WE CAN?

PRINCETON – PALMER HALL

In a sense, at Princeton we are all pussies—Princeton tigers.

Princeton – Fine Arts

SO, LITTLE PRINCETON DOESN'T WANT TO PLAY RUTGERS NO MORE?

PRINCETON – MCCORMICK HALL

RUTGERS IS LIKE A FAN—STAND IN FRONT OF IT AND GET BLOWN; STAND BEHIND IT AND GET SUCKED; STAND BESIDE IT AND GET NOTHING.

RUTGERS – BOYDEN HALL

And I thought that Rutgers sucked . . .

Temple – Beury Hall

TEMPLE IS LIKE A WHORE—YOU PAY YOUR MONEY AND GET FUCKED.

TEMPLE – BEURY HALL

The Bulletin, where no news is good news.

Temple – Annenberg Hall

6

TEMPLE FOOTBALL! ALL THE WAY TO THE SOUP BOWL!
TEMPLE – ANNENBERG HALL

WHERE IN HELL IS BROWN UNIVERSITY?
UCLA – MELNITZ HALL

Brown is on the East Coast.

Brown – Marston Hall

BROWN IS A LIBERAL SCHOOL—IT WASTES MONEY LIBERALLY.

BROWN – BARUS/HALLEY

The professors around here obviously worked their way up from the bottom—and brought it with them.
Brown – Lincoln Field Building

FORDHAM IS FOREVER!

YALE – GRADUATE SCHOOL

ROSES ARE RED.
VIOLETS ARE BLUE.
EVERYONE HERE HATES B.U.

BOSTON U – HAYDEN HALL

Amherst students without Mommy and Daddy: survival rate = 0.

Amherst – Frost Library

AMHERST SUCKS!

– *BELOW* –

AT LEAST WE CAN BUILD SOLID BUILDINGS.

AMHERST – FROST LIBRARY

As far as I'm conserned, U of Mass is far superior academicaly from Amherst.

Amherst – Frost Library

THIS LIBRARY MAKES ME SO FUCKING ANGRY. WHY DID HALF OF MY U OF MASS CAREER HAVE TO BE SPENT FIGURING OUT WHICH LIBRARY THE BOOK I WANTED WAS IN, INSTEAD OF READING THE GOD-DAMNED BOOK. IT IS TRULY A COMMENT ON THE VALUE THE STATE PUTS ON A PUBLIC EDUCATION. IF YOU WANT A QUALITY EDUCATION, THEY THINK YOU SHOULD GO TO A PRIVATE SCHOOL. DON'T TELL ME TO DO SOMETHING ABOUT IT, BECAUSE I'VE BEEN TRYING FOR YEARS. IT'S JUST SOME DAYS THAT YOU WANT TO GIVE UP.

– BELOW –

I THINK YOU'RE MAD.

U MASS – GOODELL LIBRARY

STUDYING SUCKS!

– *BELOW* –

WHY ARE YOU HERE? YOU MUST BE FUCKED UP IF YOU CAN'T HAVE A GOOD TIME AT U OF MASS.

U MASS – GOODELL LIBRARY

This building is rocked up.

–below–

. . . as well as being the ugliest piece of concrete ever foisted on the State of Massachusetts.

U Mass – Fine Arts

IF AT FIRST YOU DON'T SUCCEED, YOU ARE ABOUT AVERAGE.

– BELOW –

FIND SOMEONE TO BLAME.

– BELOW –

TRANSFER TO NYU.

NYU – VANDERBILT HALL

There are no winners at NYU, only survivors.

NYU – Biology

GET OUT WHILE THERE'S STILL TIME.

CORNELL – STIMSON HALL

"I'm an Aggie! Strong as an ox and almost as smart."

CORNELL – PLANT SCIENCES

An examination of the major fields of study gives one insight into the factors that propel students in the Northeast to success.

I am not an Aggie.

– below –

What's wrong with Aggies? If it weren't for Aggies, you would be eating your books.

Cornell – Plant Sciences

MUSIC STUDENTS ARE CYMBAL-MINDED.

U MASS – MACHMER HALL

10

Music preserves time and space.

– below –

Art preserves oil and canvas.

U Mass – Fine Arts

THIS ART DEPARTMENT BREADS ARTISTIC SCHITZOPHRINIA.

– BELOW –

. . . AND PUR SPELLIN.

U MASS – FINE ARTS

ART FOR ART'S SAKE!
MONEY FOR GOD'S SAKE!

SUNY ALBANY – FINE ARTS

Are you artists?
You are not artists. You are draftsmen, mere technicians.
Where are you going?
Where are you from?
Can you tell me? Only then are you artists.

– below –

I'm just a gift to the women of the world.

U Mass – Fine Arts

WOMEN ARTISTS SUFFER PORTFOLIO ENVY.

U MASS – FINE ARTS

Art historians are parasitical creatures who can't tell art from their assholes.

Princeton – McCormick Hall

MY ART TEACHER DOESN'T UNDERSTAND ME.

U MASS – FINE ARTS

I AM AN ARTSIE. I NEED A JOB.

CORNELL – PLANT SCIENCES

What we learn from History is that we do not learn from History.

CCNY – Wagner Hall

CAN A PLANT BE A HISTORY MAJOR?

U MASS – GOODELL HALL

Science is the not-so-slow advancement of Man into oblivion.

Cornell – Clark Science Center

LEARNING TO MOVE UP IN SCIENCE? PRACTICE HERE— PISS ON ANYTHING THAT GETS IN YOUR WAY.

HARVARD – BIOLOGICAL LABS

12

**THE SCIENTIST'S HEART IS A SEED
OF PSYCHOSIS THAT MAKES THEM ALL BLEED.
IS IT THE NEED FOR APPROVAL
OR FEAR OF REMOVAL
THAT DRIVES THEM SO HARD TO SUCCEED?**

HARVARD – BIOLOGICAL LABS

Brother Sun,
Sister Laser,
why can't I
understand the quasar?

Cornell – Clark Science Center

ASTRONOMERS ARE SPACED OUT!

U MASS – MORRILL HALL

Chem bites!

Brown – Metcalf Lab

*SIX MONTHS AGO I COON'T EVEN SPELL KEMIST AND
NOW I ARE ONE.*

BROWN – METCALF LAB

**ORGANIC CHEMISTRY IS A LEFTIST PLOT; IT'S HAD FREE
RADICALS FOR YEARS.**

DARTMOUTH – STEELE HALL

If there life after Bio 366?

Yale – Osborn Labs

PHYSIX IS PHUN!

PRINCETON – JADWIN HALL

Physics sucks!

– below –

That's why it feels so good.

Princeton – Palmer Hall

ABUSE A PHYSICS MAJOR TODAY!

– BELOW –

THEY GENERALLY PRACTICE SELF-ABUSE.

– BELOW –

PHYSICS IS SELF-ABUSE.

PRINCETON – BEGGS HALL

**TREWE WIT IS NOT YET WRITTEN
UPON THESE WALLS WHERE PHYSICISTS SHITTEN.
MAYHAPS THAT WE SHALL SOMEDAY SEE
THIR WEVE-MECHANICAL SUBTLETY.**

PRINCETON – JADWIN HALL

I'm an engineer—complex as a fusion reactor and just as compassionate.

Cornell – Plant Sciences

14

ENGINEERS ARE MERELY ADOLESCENT ZIT CASES
WITH OLDER BODIES.

U MASS – ENGINEERING EAST

**Question: How does a girl know she's sleeping with an
electrical engineering student?**
Answer: It isn't hard.

Princeton – Beggs Hall

B.S.E.'S ARE MARTYRS.

PRINCETON – BRACKETT HALL

IT'S COURSES LIKE THIS THAT KEEP THE B.S. IN B.S.E.

PRINCETON – BRACKETT HALL

Engineering Quad: Where men are men and women are too.

Princeton – Brackett Hall

RAILROAD ENGINEERS MAKE MORE MONEY THAN
ALL THE OTHERS PUT TOGETHER.

U MASS – ENGINEERING EAST

Question: How do mathematicians solve constipation?
Answer: Like anything else, they work it out with a pencil.

Penn – Dietrich Library

*IF IT SEEMS TO MAKE SENSE, IT ISN'T MATHEMATICAL
LOGIC.·*

YALE – LEET OLIVER HALL

MATHEMATICIANS DON'T SIN, THEY SINE.

– BELOW –

THAT'S WHEN THEY'RE ALONE. WHEN THEY'RE WITH SOMEONE THEY COSINE.

– BELOW –

MATHEMATICIANS ALWAYS HAVE A NICE TAN.

– BELOW –

MATHEMATICIANS ARE ALWAYS GOING OFF ON A TANGENT.

HARVARD – ROBINSON HALL

Down with revisionist mathematics.

Princeton – Student Center

NEVER TRUST A SMILING MATH PROFESSOR.

PRINCETON – PALMER HALL

The trouble with geologists is that they are always finding fault.

Penn – Wharton

MINERS ARE MORE BORING.

DARTMOUTH – WILDER

16

VIDEO PROFESSORS NEVER DIE, THEY JUST FADE TO BLACK.

TEMPLE – ANNENBERG HALL

Psychopharmacology is a joke!

SUNY Albany – Social Science

URBAN PLANNERS EAT THEIR DEAD.

COLUMBIA

Once I lived a life of peace, ease and comfort; now I'm a pre-med student.

Amherst – Frost Library

QUESTION: WHY DID THE PRE-MED STUDENT CROSS THE ROAD?
ANSWER: BECAUSE IT WAS TOO FAR TO YA-ELL.

PRINCETON – BEGGS HALL

**THERE ONCE WAS A YOUNG LAWYER FROM YALE
WHO LET IT HANG OUT LIKE A TAIL.
AND A SEXY TORTFEASOR
WHO THOUGHT IT WOULD PLEASE HER
CUT IT OFF WITHOUT EVEN A QUAIL.**

GRATIS DICTUM

YALE – LAW

Old lawyers never die, they just lose their appeal.

Columbia – Law

YALE LAW STUDENTS MUST FIRST LEARN HOW TO
BUDGET THEIR TIME EFFECTIVELY, ALLOCATING MOST
OF THEIR TIME TO STUDYING THE LAW WHILE
RESERVING SOME TIME FOR FUCKING.

YALE – LAW

Having trouble sleeping? Try accounting.

SUNY Albany – Library

*PEOPLE IN BUSINESS SCHOOL DON'T GIVE A DAMN
ABOUT ANYTHING EXCEPT BUCKS.*

TEMPLE – PALEY LIBRARY

**THE MBA—TOO MUCH WORK TO GET IT, TOO LITTLE
WORK AFTER YOU GET IT.**

***BOSTON COLLEGE – MCGUINN
HALL***

Sociology is the opiate of all classes.

Yale – Dunham Lab

PhD—PURE HUMAN DUNG.

*COLUMBIA – INTERNATIONAL
AFFAIRS*

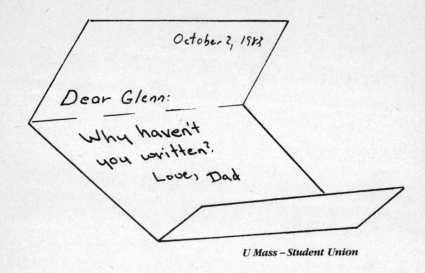

U Mass – Student Union

Whatever the attributes of the college or the major field, what really counts is obviously the makeup of the Northeastern student himself. We found varying opinions of student life in the Northeast.

THE INCOMING FRESHMEN CAN'T EVEN WRITE WELL ENGLISH.

TEMPLE – PALEY LIBRARY

SCHOOL DOES MAKE YOU SMART; I'M STILL SMARTING FROM MY LAST EXAM.

NYU – SHEPARD HALL

Help! Exams!
Help the world!

Smith – Hillyer Hall

EXAMS ARE AN ENVIRONMENTAL HAZARD.

NYU – BOBST LIBRARY

How does one get on the endangered species list?

CCNY – Eisner Hall

I JUST TOOK MY THIRD FINAL, AND AM I HAPPY!

BOSTON U – STONE SCIENCE BUILDING

MAKE SCHOOL EASIER!

SUNY ALBANY – BUSINESS ADMINISTRATION

I'm mad as hell, and I can't take it any longer.

U Mass – Goodell Library

IF YOU THINK THAT SCHOOL IS TOUGH, WAIT UNTIL YOU START WORKING.

DARTMOUTH – BAKER HALL

I just wanna be understood, feared in my neighborhood.

Princeton – McCosh Hall

20

*WE OURSELVES ARE THE POWER THEY DENY US; RISE
UP AND CONQUER!*

CORNELL – LINCOLN HALL

IF DOGS RUN FREE, WHY CAN'T WE?

HARVARD – BOYLSTON HALL

"Do what thou wilt," shall be the whole of the law.

Princeton – Palmer Hall

WHITE-COLLAR CONSERVATIVE POINTING HIS
PLASTIC FINGER AT ME, HOPING MY KIND WILL DROP
AND DIE, BUT I'M GONNA KEEP MY FREAK FLAG HIGH.

U MASS – ENGINEERING EAST

There are times when I wonder about all this.

CCNY – Cohen Library

*I'M SITTING HERE INSIDE THIS STALL, WHICH IS A
SMALL SECTION OF THIS ROOM, WHICH IS A MINOR PORTION
OF THIS BUILDING, WHICH IS HARDLY NOTICEABLE AMONG
THE MANY IN THIS CITY, WHICH IS A DOT ON THE MAP OF
THIS COUNTRY, WHICH IS ONLY A CORNER OF THIS
PLANET, WHICH SPINS UNNOTICED WITHIN THIS SOLAR
SYSTEM, WHICH IS NOTHING WITHIN THIS UNIVERSE, AND
I AM WORRIED ABOUT A ZIT ON MY NOSE.*

NYU – BOBST LIBRARY

ALL IN ALL WE'RE JUST ANOTHER PRICK IN THE WALL.
AMHERST – FROST LIBRARY

We are often wrong and remarkably ineffective.
Harvard – Widener Library

AS A STUDENT YOU HAVE AN INALIENABLE RIGHT TO WAIT IN LINE.
CCNY – FINLEY HALL

College is like a woman—you work so hard to get in, and after nine months you wish you had never come.
Penn – Dietrich Library

LORD, HELP US OUT OF THIS DUMP.

– BELOW –

HELP YOURSELVES.
U MASS – FINE ARTS

I WISH THAT I COULD BE DECISIVE. THEN I'D UNDERSTAND WHERE LIFE IS FOR ME.
U MASS – GOODELL LIBRARY

Death! Doom! Gloom! Despair! Agony! & Me!
Princeton – McCosh Hall

LIE LOW, STAY HIDDEN, AND CONCEAL THE WAY YOU THINK, THE THINGS YOU FEEL.

YALE – LAW

I am in great pain. My girlfriend broke up with me after five months of what I thought was a great relationship. She used me. She never gave me a reason for breaking up. She doesn't even talk to me now.

URI – Library

THANK GOD THERE'S WATER TO DROWN IN.

U MASS – BARTLETT

HELP ME!

U MASS – GOODELL LIBRARY

I'm so lonely. I've got to find somebody to love.

URI – Library

WHY DON'T YOU ALL STOP WORRYING ABOUT YOURSELVES AND JUST TRY TO ENJOY LIFE. IF YOU'RE REALLY COMFY WITH LIFE, YOU DON'T HAVE TO ADVERTISE ON BATHROOM WALLS.

RADCLIFFE/HARVARD –LEHMAN HALL

You feel unwanted? Left-out? Have you considered defenestration?

– below –

I prefer precipitation.

Harvard – Biological Lab

SOMETIMES I WISH EVERYONE WOULD JUST LEAVE ME ALONE.

BOSTON COLLEGE – MCGUINN

KILL ME BEFORE I STOP AGAIN!

U MASS – FINE ARTS

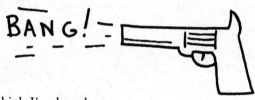

I think I've lost the game.

– below –

Please keep trying.

U Mass – Fine arts

I grow old.
I grow old.

Penn – Bennet Hall

I feel so ancient.

URI – Memorial Union

OLDER IS BETTER.

> *SUNY ALBANY – BUSINESS*
> *ADMINISTRATION*

SOMEONE WAKE ME WHEN IT'S OVER.

> ***COLUMBIA***

Quiet down, I want to sleep.

> *Princeton – McCosh Hall*

THERE'S NO WAY OUT OF HERE, WHEN YOU'RE IN, YOU'RE IN FOR GOOD.

> *COLUMBIA*

Go mental!

> ***Amherst – Frost Library***

I'M NOT LIVING IN THE REAL WORLD; REALLY, I'M LOST.

> *– BELOW –*

JOIN THE CLUB.

> *U MASS – GOODELL LIBRARY*

I'M SO FUCKIN' CRAZY, I'LL NEVER GET PAST 19.

> ***U MASS – FINE ARTS***

The symptoms of my disease is not the disease, the disease is my symptoms.

Radcliffe/Harvard – Science Center

IT'S SO NICE TO BE INSANE, NO ONE ASKS TO EXPLAIN.

U MASS – GOODELL LIBRARY

I know what I want but I just don't know how to go about getting it.

U Mass – Goodell Library

IS THERE LIFE AFTER COLLEGE?

CORNELL – PLANT SCIENCES

AS I APPROACH MY SENIOR YEAR I FIND THAT MY EDUCATION HAS BENEFITED MY PARENTS AS WELL; THEY MAKE MORE SENSE EVERY DAY.

HARVARD – BIOLOGICAL LABS

Hello Mom, send money.

(in phone cubicle)
Radcliffe/Harvard – Lehman Hall

If God had meant for Preppies to be engineers he would have put calculators on their gator shirts.

PRINCETON – BRACKETT HALL

Students in the Northeast are quick to show appreciation for various members of the student body.

Question: How many Preppies does it take to screw in a light bulb?
Answer: Two—one to get the Diet Pepsi and one to call Daddy.

Temple – Student Activities Center

QUESTION: WHAT IS A PREPPIE'S FIRST TOY?
ANSWER: A CAMARO WITH TRAINING WHEELS.

TEMPLE – STUDENT ACTIVITIES CENTER

THANK GOD IT'S SUMMER AND ALL THE LITTLE TWITS ARE GONE.

TEMPLE – ANNENBERG HALL

The typical young Princeton snot
sponges off Daddy a lot.
And he thinks his remittance
a pauper's poor pittance.
The thought makes his brain cells all clot.

Princeton – Fine Hall

FRATS ARE BASICALLY HOUSES OF INSECURE
DOUCHE BAGS.

CORNELL – ROCKEFELLER HALL

Question: How do you tell a Princeton girl?
Answer: She's the one with braided armpits.

Princeton – Palmer Hall

PRINCETON GIRLS DO NOT HAVE LIBIDOS, THEY HAVE
SWEATERS.

PRINCETON – FINE HALL

DEAR GUYS: WHY ARE PRINCETON GUYS SUCH
SCHMUCKS? ALL THEY WANT IS A GOOD LAY. WHY CAN'T
THEY TREAT WOMEN AS PEOPLE—AS HUMAN BEINGS WITH
LIVES AND THOUGHTS AND MORALS AND INTEGRITY AND
SELF-RESPECT OF THEIR OWN?

PRINCETON – FINE HALL

Penn women are for Penn men who are too lazy to masturbate.

Penn – Wharton

WHY ARE PENN WOMEN SO GOOD LOOKING?

– BELOW –

BECAUSE THEY WORKED IN STEEL MILLS ALL THEIR LIVES.

– BELOW –

BECAUSE THEY GOT HIT WITH BAGS OF NICKELS.

– BELOW –

THEY HAD THE LEAD IN "THE EXORCIST."

– BELOW –

THEY'VE HAD GOOD FOOD, WARM HOUSES AND DOCTORS ALL THEIR LIVES.

– BELOW –

PLASTIC SURGERY WITH CHAINS.

– BELOW –

YOU'RE LOOKING AT THE WRONG END.

– BELOW –

WHEN THEY WERE LITTLE, THEIR MOTHERS FED THEM HARD BEANS WITH A SLING SHOT.

– BELOW –

ASK PLAYBOY.

– BELOW –

WHY IS THE SWIMMING POOL CALLED THE "BAY OF PIGS?"

– BELOW –

THEY ARE UGLY ENOUGH TO MAKE FREIGHT TRAINS TAKE DIRT ROADS.

– BELOW –

KEEPING THEIR NOSES SO HIGH HAS CAUSED OZONE BURNS.

– BELOW –

PENN GIRLS HAVE LOOKS; PENN STATE GIRLS HAVE THE BRAINS.

PENN – DIETRICH LIBRARY

Question: What's the difference between a Penn girl and an elephant?
Answer: ????

Penn – Bennet Hall

Love is like a shoe,
you should try it on
before buying.

BOSTON COLLEGE – MCQUINN
HALL

Sometimes the appreciations of the student body become more narrowed and more serious.

Once in a while I would look at you and see the twinkle in your eyes.

Dartmouth – Baker Hall

THE SECOND DAY OF MY 19TH YEAR AND WHAT A WONDERFUL WORLD IT IS—WITH FLOWERS AND BLUE SKIES AND, MOST OF ALL, MEN!

RADCLIFFE/HARVARD – SCIENCE CENTER

ENTWINE WITH THE RIGHT WINE.

CORNELL – MCGRAW HALL

Love you'ns!

Harvard – Emerson Hall

I LOVE US.

CCNY – FINLEY HALL

Love is what you make of it.

Cornell – Plant Sciences

THE GUYS AT THIS SCHOOL ARE FAR TOO BLATANT.
U MASS – GOODELL LIBRARY

TOMMY, CALL ME, CUZ I LOVE YOUR ASS!

U MASS – GOODELL LIBRARY

Love comes in spurts.

Cornell – Plant Sciences

YOU'RE MY EVERY WET DREAM COME TRUE.

U MASS – GOODELL LIBRARY

It's not easy being a sex symbol.

One would expect students to write most about that field in which they hope to find the greatest success. They write a great deal about sex.

**The more I think about sex,
the more I think about sex.**

SEX IS LIKE SNOW—NO TWO PIECES THE SAME.

SEX IS MEANINGLESS WITHOUT RECOMBINATION.

$$Se^x = f(u)^n + v(d)$$

Princeton – Fine Hall

I GOT V.D., AND YOU DON'T! HA! HA!

BOSTON U – HAYDEN HALL

If sex is a pain in the ass you're doing it the wrong way.

Boston College – Higgens Hall

KISS ME! I'M HORNY!

PENN – RITTENBERG LAB

WHAT DO WE WANT? SEX!
WHEN DO WE WANT IT? NOW!
HOW DO WE WANT IT? LONG AND HARD!

PRINCETON – MCCOSH HALL

Lust is the root of all life.

Princeton – McCosh Hall

THEY ARE SUBJECT TO THEIR DESIRES, AND THEIR DESIRES RULE OVER THEM.

URI – LIBRARY

34

Some folks need the killer weed.
Some folks need cocaine.
Some folks need a little speed
to purify the brain.
Some folks need two women.
Some need alcohol.
Everyone needs something.
Lord, I need to ball.

Boston U – Stone Science Building

STANDING ON THE VERGE OF GETTING IT ON.
TEMPLE – ANNENBERG HALL

I WANT TO GET IT ON WITH YOU.
U MASS – FINE ARTS

Live a little, have an orgasm.
Penn – Rittenberg Lab

SCREW

– BELOW –

LOVE TO!

– BELOW –

PLEASE, NOT HERE; I'M TRYING TO STUDY.
AMHERST – FROST LIBRARY

When in doubt, whip it out!

U Mass – Machmer Hall

MAKE LOVE, NOT LAW REVIEW

– BELOW –

ARE THEY MUTUALLY EXCLUSIVE?

BOSTON U – LAW BUILDING

WHY IS IT THAT GIRLS USE SEX TO GET LOVE AND BOYS USE LOVE TO GET SEX?

U MASS – ENGINEERING EAST

A good piece of ass is hard to get but easy to come by.

Brown – Barus/Halley Hall

$b^4 i^4 q, uqt, \dfrac{ru}{18}$?

PRINCETON – BEGGS HALL

She offered her honor.
I honored her offer.
So, all night long
it was 'on her' and 'off her'.

Classic on all campuses

VA-GI-NA (VA JI´ NA), N. 1. THE BOX A PENIS COMES IN

PRINCETON – MCCOSH HALL

DO YOU REALIZE THAT SINCE THE AVERAGE VAGINA IS SEVEN INCHES LONG AND THE AVERAGE PENIS IS SIX INCHES LONG, THERE ARE HUNDREDS OF MILES OF WASTED VAGINA?

PRINCETON – MCCORMICK HALL

There once was a man from Penn
who could do it again and again.
His prick was immense,
and we watched with suspense
as he screwed number one hundred ten.

Penn – Rittenberg Lab

IF LIGHT SLEEPERS GO TO BED WITH A LIGHT ON, WHAT DO HARD SLEEPERS GO TO BED WITH?

RUTGERS – BOYDEN LAB

**Long or short, thick or thin,
Vaseline will get it in.**

Temple – Curtis Hall

*MORE THAN A HANDFUL IS A WASTE.
LESS THAN A HANDFUL IS A SHAME.*

PENN – WHARTON

IT'S NOT THE SIZE OF THE MISSILE, BUT THE ACCURACY OF ITS GUIDANCE SYSTEM THAT MAKES IT EFFECTIVE

BOSTON U – STONE SCIENCE BUILDING

Sex discriminates against the shy and ugly.

Boston College – Higgins Hall

WHICH OF US IS THE OPPOSITE SEX?

COLUMBIA – URIS HALL

National Sex Week—don't let your meat loaf.

Penn – Bennet Hall

BRVTVS FORNICATVS

*SUNY ALBANY – BUSINESS
ADMINISTRATION*

FUCKING IS SO MUCH FUN. WHY DON'T WE ALL DO IT
MORE OFTEN?

AMHERST – FROST LIBRARY

I haven't had sex in a month. I'm dying. I don't know how
virgins can stand it.

U Mass – Bartlett Hall

VIRGINITY IS LIKE A BALLOON—ALL IT NEEDS IS
ONE PRICK AND IT'S GONE.

*BOSTON COLLEGE – FULTON
HALL*

To all virgins: 'Thanks for nothing!'

U Mass – Bartlett

JOIN THE MORAL MAJORITY NOW!

– BELOW –

THE IMMORAL MINORITY IS MORE FUN.

SUNY ALBANY – LIBRARY

IF WE CAN DO IT, IT'S NOT IMMORAL.

DARTMOUTH – BAKER HALL

Legalize necrophilia!

Cornell – Rockefeller Hall

SEX IS LIKE BRIDGE—IF YOU DON'T HAVE A GOOD PARTNER, YOU NEED A GOOD HAND OF YOUR OWN.

BROWN – BARUS/HALLEY

If God had intended for us not to masturbate He would have made our arms shorter.

Penn – Williams Hall

IF YOU WIPE MORE THAN ONCE, YOU'RE PLAYING WITH IT.

NYU – MEYER HALL

YOU CAN PRICK YOUR FINGER, BUT PLEASE DON'T FINGER YOUR PRICK.

SUNY ALBANY – LEARNING
CENTER

If you keep your head on your shoulders you might get sperm on your shirt.

U Mass – Fine Arts

THE ENGLISHMAN SAID, "TWO HANDS ON THE BIRD ARE WORTH ONE IN THE BUSH."

PRINCETON – EAST PYNE

Castrate rapists!

– below –

Plug up dikes!

– below –

It's dykes, stupid!

U Mass – Goodell Library

JOIN THE NAVY AND RIDE THE WAVES.

PRINCETON – GUYOT HALL

TRY CELIBACY—DON'T FUCK IF IT BORES YOU.

CCNY – SCIENCE HALL

40

Men who pull out too fast leave rubber.

U Mass – Goodell Library

FUCK ONANISM!

COLUMBIA – PUPIN HALL

MY NOOKIE DAYS ARE OVER.
MY PILOT LIGHT IS OUT.
WHAT USED TO BE MY SEX APPEAL
IS NOW MY WATER SPOUT.

IT USED TO BE EMBARRASSING,
THE WAY IT WOULD BEHAVE,
HOW EACH AND EVERY MORNING
IT WOULD STAND AND WATCH ME SHAVE.

NOW IT IS DEPRESSING
AND GIVES ME OLD-AGE BLUES,
HOW IT HANGS ITS LITTLE HEAD
AND WATCHES ME TIE MY SHOES.

TEMPLE – STUDENT ACTIVITIES
CENTER

It is better to burn out than rust out.

URI – Kelly Hall

HARVARD – BIOLOGICAL LABS

Despite the need to concentrate on their studies, students in the Northeast still find time to devote to the preservation of "natural" resources.

Save a mouse; eat a pussy.

Temple – Beury Hall

IF GOD HAD NOT INTENDED MAN TO EAT PUSSY, WHY'D HE MAKE IT LOOK LIKE A TACO?

TEMPLE – CURTIS HALL

MARCVS CVNNILINGVS

SUNY ALBANY – LIBRARY

Sit on a happy face!

SUNY Albany – Library

I LOVE 'EM IN FRILLS.
I LOVE 'EM IN LACE.
I LOVE 'EM THE BEST
WHEN THEY SIT ON MY FACE.

PRINCETON – GUYOT HALL

There are only two things in the world that smell like fish, one is fish.

Princeton – Guyot Hall

HERE'S TO THE CRACK THAT NEVER HEALS.
THE MORE YOU RUB THE BETTER IT FEELS.
THERE IS NO SOAP THIS SIDE OF HELL
THAT WILL TAKE AWAY THAT FISHY SMELL.

URI – RESOURCE DEVELOPMENT
CENTER

FISH IS GIVING PUSSY A BAD NAME.

TEMPLE – CURTIS

Everything more or less tastes like tuna fish.

NYU – Barney Building

OYSTERS HAVE MORE FUN.

HARVARD – BIOLOGICAL LABS

Lick-a-dee-clit!

U Mass – Goodell

DOMINICVS
CLITORIS

*SUNY ALBANY – BUSINESS
ADMINISTRATION*

**HE GAVE THE LADIES A LICK AND A PROMISE, AND THE
LADIES GAVE HIM A KICK IN THE GROIN.**

U MASS – GOODELL LIBRARY

I want my head! I want it now!
I want my head while I'm in bed!

U Mass – Goodell Library

A COCKSUCKER IS NOT A BAD MAN; IT'S A GOOD
WOMAN.

PENN – RITTENBERG LAB

Do people who do it have more fun?

U MASS – FINE ARTS

Major philosophical questions sometimes confront the aspiring student.

Professors do it with class.

Princeton – Guyot Hall

ENGINEERS DO IT WITH MORE PRECISION.

U MASS – FINE ARTS

Chemical engineers do it in stages.

U Mass – Student Union

BASS FISHERMEN HAVE STIFFER RODS.

DARTMOUTH – WILDER HALL

DOING IT WITH AN ELECTRICAL ENGINEER IS A SHOCKING EXPERIENCE.

U MASS – ENGINEERING EAST

Electrical engineers do it sinosodically.

– below –

Yeh, off and on.

U Mass – Engineering East

PHYSICISTS DO IT WITH HIGH ENERGY AND NON-SIMPLE HARMONIC MOTION.

TEMPLE – BARTON HALL

Chemists make better lovers because they have had more experience with 'i-ons' and they know where your free radicals are.

SUNY Albany – Chemistry

PSYCH MAJORS DO IT ON THE COUCH.

U MASS – MORRILL HALL

WOMEN PHILOSOPHY MAJORS HAVE BETTER FOUNDATIONS.

HARVARD – EMERSON HALL

"Homosexuality is not so bad," said Bill, half in Ernest.

PRINCETON – FINE HALL

There are choices to be made.

I'm a homo; how does that grab you?

SUNY Albany – Library

SODOMY IS A PAIN IN THE ASS.

YALE – BECTON CENTER

 Sappho People

RADCLIFFE/HARVARD – LEHMAN HALL

Did you know that some plants are gay? They deny it at first, but that is the root of their problem.

U Mass – Goodell Library

BLOW JOB ANYONE?

– BELOW –

WHAT HAPPENED TO GOOD OLD FUCKING?

HARVARD – GEORGE GUND HALL

Jesus Christ, guys! What ever happened to good old-fashioned heterosexual bathroom wall yearnings for warm, wild and wet romps and humps with fair and horny members of the opposite sex?

Penn – Dietrich Library

DON'T STRAIGHTS EVER SHIT, OR IS WRITING ON WALLS A HOMOSEXUAL TRAIT? OOOOPS!

YALE – WOOLSEY HALL

THE ODDS ARE 10 TO 1 THAT THE ODDS ARE WRONG.

SUNY ALBANY – FINE ARTS

Gays unite!

– below –

So we can get you all at one time.

Cornell – Rockefeller Hall

48

Lesbianism is not unrelated to feminism, but neither is it the purest form. Lesbians and straight women, both equally committed to feminism, must work together. One is not at all a better feminist for being a lesbian or condemning lesbianism.

Radcliffe/Harvard – Lebman Hall

DYKES ARE REALLY FUCKED UP ALL THE TIME.

– BELOW –

SORRY, SWEETHEART, DYKES DON'T FUCK. DON'T GET US MIXED UP WITH YOUR HET IDEOLOGIES.

RADCLIFFE/HARVARD –
GOODELL LIBRARY

My uncle is a closet homosapien!

NYU – Vanderbilt Hall

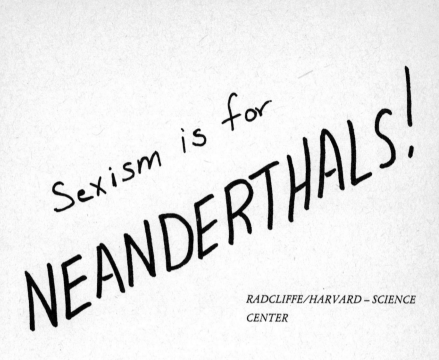

Sexism is for NEANDERTHALS!

RADCLIFFE/HARVARD – SCIENCE CENTER

Some things must be dealt with seriously.

Love your sisters; love yourself.

– below –

Love your brothers.

Radcliffe/Harvard – Lehman Hall

WOMEN WHO WANT TO BE THE EQUALS OF MEN LACK AMBITION.

—WRITTEN BY A HETEROSEXUAL
U MASS – GOODELL LIBRARY

50

BROTHERS—RESPECT YOUR SISTERS.

> *RADCLIFFE/HARVARD – LEHMAN HALL*

There are no bitches, only Sisters in terrible situations.

> *U Mass – Herter Hall*

MISSIONARY STYLE IS BEST FOR WOMEN BECAUSE THAT'S THE WAY YOU'LL STAY.

– BELOW –

WE'RE NOT, BUT MEN WOULD LIKE TO KEEP US THAT WAY.

– BELOW –

THE TRUTH IS WHAT YOU WANT TO BELIEVE.

> *RADCLIFFE/HARVARD – LEHMAN HALL*

Wear cotton underwear!

> *NYU – Biology*

ABORTION IS A CRUEL NECESSITY IN A LIFE WITHOUT PRIMARY CHOICE.

– BELOW –

WHAT IS MORE IMPORTANT—A WOMAN OR A MASS OF CELLS?

> *RADCLIFFE/HARVARD – EMERSON HALL*

*SIGN: "SANITARY NAPKINS AND TAMPONS ARE
AVAILABLE IN THE STOCKROOM BASEMENT LEVEL MON–FRI 9
AM TO 4:30 PM."*
(BENEATH)
**ALL WOMEN WILL SCHEDULE THE START OF THEIR
PERIODS TO COINCIDE WITH THESE TIMES.**

*RADCLIFFE/HARVARD – SCIENCE
CENTER*

Use tree bark . . . just don't use tampons.

– below –

Oh, come off it! That's what the men who control the billion
dollar tampon industries want you to believe. If you boil a sea
sponge for 1–3 minutes it'll be perfectly safe. It's that simple. Have
you noticed that they won't let us buy speculums without a
prescription now too? Sense a pattern?

Smith – Steele Hall

NO NUKES FOR MEN.

U MASS – STUDENT CENTER

Women's liberation is the main cause.

– below –

Wrong! People's liberation is the mainer cause.

Amherst – Frost Library.

A man's
success
is judged
by the
type of
drugs he
uses.

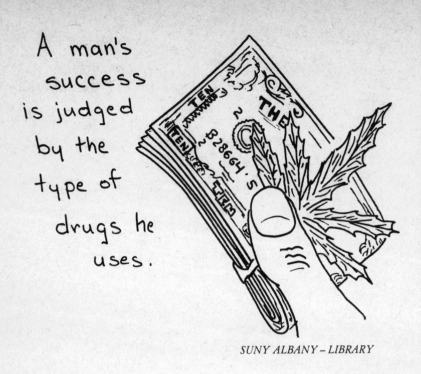

SUNY ALBANY – LIBRARY

Evidence shows that students in the Northeast are actively preparing to be judged.

ACID, A GREAT TRIP!

– BELOW –

BUT NOT THE TRIP TO HELL! THAT'S WHAT YOU HAVE TO LIVE AFTERWARDS.

HARVARD – BIOLOGICAL LABS

Opium is the religion of the masses.

Princeton – Woolworth Center

A WORLD WITHOUT MUSIC IS LIKE A WORLD WITHOUT COCAINE.

COLUMBIA

Reality is for people who can't handle drugs.

Princeton – Student Center

PEOPLE WITH A HIGH I.Q. HIT THE TOP. WHY DON'T YOU?

– BELOW –

PEOPLE WITH A HIGH HIT IT FASTER.

SUNY ALBANY – LECTURE CENTER

SELL DRUGS, NOT WAR.

PRINCETON – MCCOSH HALL

Pot heads are New Jersey burnouts.

Boston College – McGuinn Hall

IF TIME IS A WASTE OF LIFE AND LIFE IS A WASTE OF TIME, THEN GET WASTED AND HAVE THE TIME OF YOUR LIFE.

URI – LIBRARY

LET'S GET SMASHED.

> *RADCLIFFE/HARVARD – LEHMAN*
> *HALL*

The Heineken Uncertainty Principle: You cannot be sure how many beers you had last night.

> *SUNY Albany – Chemistry*

I CAN REALLY CONVERSE WITH HIRAM WALKER; HE UNDERSTANDS WHAT MOTIVATES ME.

> *YALE–STERLING LIBRARY*

Can a plant be alcoholic?

> *U Mass – Goodell Library*

DRUGS
and
SEX
and
ROCK 'N ROLL!

HARVARD – GEORGE GUND HALL

Having considered the importance of drugs and sex, we could not ignore the impact of rock 'n' roll.

I MAY BE DUMB, BECAUSE I KNOW I'M NOT SMART, BUT DEEP DOWN INSIDE I'VE GOT A ROCK 'N' ROLL HEART.

PRINCETON – STUDENT CENTER

What America needs is disco and soul. To Hell with rock 'n' roll.

Rutgers – Conklin Hall

DEATH BEFORE DISCO!

URI – LIBRARY

Boogie till ya puke!

– below –

Bop till ya drop!

– below –

Shake till ya break!

SUNY Albany – Library

BETTER MUSIC THROUGH VIOLENCE.

CORNELL – GOODWIN SMITH HALL

Lennon lives 4EVA!

PEACE LOVERS UNITE!

Let there be peace.

RADCLIFFE/HARVARD – SCIENCE CENTER

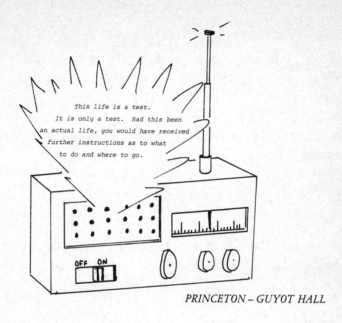

This life is a test.
It is only a test. Had this been
an actual life, you would have received
further instructions as to what
to do and where to go.

PRINCETON – GUYOT HALL

Perhaps one factor in the Northeast student's triumphs is his understanding of life. Numerous understandings were expressed.

LIFE IS LIKE A GAME OF POOL, THE MAN WITH THE MOST BALLS IN HIS POCKETS WINS.

U MASS – ENGINEERING EAST

Life is like a game of pinball—you win or you lose your balls.

Dartmouth – Wilder Hall

LIFE IS A PLACEBO.

BROWN – METCALF LAB

Is there life after birth?

Yale-Law

OKAY, LIFE, HIT ME WITH YOUR BEST SHOT.

TEMPLE – ANNENBERG HALL

LIFE IS LIKE A HORSE'S ASS—SOMETIMES IT REALLY STINKS!

SUNY ALBANY – LEARNING
CENTER

Life is an asshole. You can try anything you like to make it better but still nothing comes out but shit. —An optimist.

–below–

P.S. If you still want to try life after reading this, you better start liking shit.

Radcliffe/Harvard – Emerson Hall

IT'S MY LIFE AND I'LL DO WHAT I WANT.

–BELOW–

WHO'S STOPPING YOU?

–BELOW–

I DON'T KNOW WHAT I WANT.

–BELOW–

WELL THEN, HOW THE FUCK ARE WE SUPPOSED TO KNOW?

–BELOW–

GO WEST.

U MASS – GOODELL LIBRARY

Life is like a penis; when it's soft you can't beat it, but when it's hard you get fucked.

Princeton – Green Hall

THE STRESS OF LIFE IS KILLING ME.

SUNY ALBANY–LIBRARY

YOUR LIFE WILL GET WORSE BEFORE IT GETS BETTER.

–BELOW–

WHO SAID IT WILL GET BETTER.

COLUMBIA – JOURNALISM

Life can be at its best when it's at its worst.

Boston College – Fulton Hall

THE WORTH OF SOCIETY HAS DWINDLED TO NONEXISTENCE; HUMAN NATURE IS THAT OF A BARBARIAN, TRUST IS ARCHAIC, PEACE OF MIND IS IMPOSSIBLE, YET LIFE GOES ON.

U MASS – FINE ARTS

60

Life is a contradiction.

–below–

It is *not!*

Penn – Williams Hall

LIFE IS AN ILLUSION CREATED BY A BEING WHICH HAS NO BETTER WAY OF EXPLAINING ITSELF.

DARTMOUTH – WILDER HALL

ALL LIFE WE WORK, BUT WORK'S A BORE.
IF LIFE'S FOR LIVING, WHAT'S LIVING FOR?

U MASS – GOODELL LIBRARY

Ah, sweet mystery of Life, at last I've found you.

Yale – Law

LIFE IS KNOWING WHEN TO MAKE A GRACEFUL EXIT.

PENN – DIETRICH LIBRARY

Listen to God before your candle burns out!

Temple – Paley Library

The evidence of religion's role in the student's success is less than conclusive in the Northeast.

JESUS IS COMING!

–BELOW–

WE'LL GET HIM AGAIN.

COLUMBIA – FAYERWEATHER HALL

LORD OF LIGHT, INC.

U MASS – BARTLETT HALL

62

God is not dead, I saw him just yesterday.

Boston College – McGuinn

GOD IS THE ANSWER!

– BELOW –

WHAT IS THE QUESTION?

– BELOW –

WHAT IS 'DOG' SPELLED BACKWARDS?

HARVARD – BIOLOGICAL LABS

God speaks softly, but carries the stick.

Temple – Paley Library

GOD IS BIG DADDY!

CORNELL – FRANKLIN HALL

AN HONEST GOD IS THE NOBLEST WORK OF MAN.

PRINCETON—BEGGS HALL

When was the last time that you got in touch with God?

– BELOW –

Living is being in touch with God.

Temple – Paley Library

RELIGION IS THE OPIATE OF THE MASSES.

– BELOW –

MASS IS THE RELIGION OF THE OPIATES.

PRINCETON – WOOLWORTH
CENTER

If you haven't figured out why God has ignored this planet for the past six centuries, there's no hope for you.

If you think God will continue to ignore this planet for the next twenty to forty years, there's no hope for you.

But if you listen to what your planet has to say, you are truly a child of God.

Cornell – Goodwin Smith Hall

JESUS IS THE ONLY ANSWER TO YOUR PROBLEM. TALK TO HIM TODAY.

– BELOW –

$$OKAY, J. C., SOLVE: \frac{4^e \times 2}{sine^2 \times Cos\ 3 \times 4^x}$$

SUNY ALBANY – HUMANITIES

GOD CAME HERE IN PRE-MED, BUT SWITCHED TO GEOLOGY. HE MADE THE EARTH FOR SENIOR THESIS.

– BELOW –

B+

PRINCETON – FINE HALL

The meek shall inherit the Earth, but they're gonna have to fight for it.

A student in the Northeast has carefully examined and catalogued certain truths to carry with him into later ventures. Perhaps these account for his prosperity.

BEWARE THE CALCULATIONS OF THE MEEK, WHO GAMBLED NOTHING, GAVE NOTHING, AND COULD NEVER RECEIVE ENOUGH.

Winning isn't everything, but losing sure sucks!

*TO THINE OWN SELF BE TRUE. (IF NOT THAT, AT
LEAST MAKE SOME MONEY.)*

SUNY ALBANY – HUMANITIES

YOU CAN FOOL SOME OF THE PEOPLE ONCE.

PRINCETON – GUYOT HALL

If it's worth doing, it's worth doing for money.

CCNY – Wagner Hall

SUCCESS IS COUNTED SWEETEST BY THOSE WHO
NEVER SUCCEED.

U MASS – GOODELL HALL

**We all go through Life thinking that we can never do
anything great, not knowing all along that we are right.**

Princeton – Woolworth Center

HE JESTS AT SCARS WHO NEVER FELT A WOUND.

CORNELL – PLANT SCIENCES

**WORK HARD, BE HONEST, LOVE PEOPLE—THAT, MY
FRIEND, IS THE ANSWER.**

TEMPLE – BEURY HALL

Trifles make perfection, and perfection is no trifle.

U Mass – Engineering East

SMILE AND THE WORLD SMILES WITH YOU.

U MASS – STOCKBRIDGE HALL

Character is the compass of Life.

U Mass – Machmer Hall

PREJUDICE SUCKS!

CORNELL – GOOOWIN SMITH HALL

I AIN'T PREJUDICED—I HATE EVERYONE EQUALLY. J.R.

TEMPLE – BARTON HALL

Bigots come in all colors, shapes and sizes.

Temple – Barton Hall

THOSE WHO DEHUMANIZE OTHERS LOSE THEIR OWN HUMANENESS IN THE PROCESS.

AMHERST – FROST LIBRARY

Man's greatest error is prejudice. His second greatest mistake is putting up bathroom walls to write it on.

Temple – Speakman Hall

AMAZING! A WALL WITHOUT ANY RACIST OR SEXIST REMARKS.

– BELOW –

GAY NIGGERS SUCK!

– BELOW –

I HATE GAY CHINKS!

PENN – WILLIAMS HALL

BLACKS HAVE DISCRIMINATED AGAINST WHITES TOO— THEY NEVER LET US BE THE SLAVES.

BOSTON COLLEGE – FULTON HALL

Beauty is only skin deep, but ugliness goes down to the bone.

Brown – Barus/Halley

OPINIONS ARE LIKE ASSHOLES, EVERYONE HAS ONE.

RADCLIFFE/HARVARD – EMERSON HALL

Some folks look for answers, others look for fights.

U Mass – Goodell Library

GETTING WHACKED ON THE HEAD WITH A CARROT CAN HURT AS MUCH AS A STICK.

CCNY – FINLEY HALL

DIPLOMACY: THE ART OF LETTING THE OTHER GUY HAVE YOUR WAY.

PRINCETON – GREEN HALL

Man is the point where Time and Eternity meet and their fine point of contact is called forgiveness.

– below –

If anyone really understands that, tell me what it means.

U Mass – Fine Arts

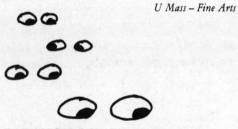

EVEN PARANOIDS HAVE ENEMIES

COLUMBIA – AVERY HALL

Psychotics build castles in the air.
Neurotics live in them.
Psychologists collect the rent.

Princeton – Green Hall

CASTLES MADE OF SAND SLIP INTO THE SEA EVENTUALLY.

AMHERST – FROST LIBRARY

CENSORSHIP IS THE FIRST REFUGE OF THE LIAR.

URI – KELLY HALL

Is the axiom of choice true?

U Mass – Engineering East

TRUTH IS A PERSON WHO WAS, AND IS, AND ALWAYS WILL BE.

HARVARD – EMERSON HALL

Sometimes I think we are alone. Sometimes I think we are not. Either way, the thought is staggering.

Dartmouth – Wilder Hall

CLONING IS THE HIGHEST FORM OF FLATTERY.

BOSTON U – HAYDEN HALL

A MAN IS A SLAVE THAT IS LIVING FOR SOMETHING OTHER THAN HIS SELF.

PRINCETON – WOOLWORTH CENTER

Treachery: to approach in the guise of trust and betray. There is no other root of evil.

Princeton – Green Hall

POETRY: A BRIEF DECLAMATION OF ONE MAN'S FRUSTRATIONS.

U MASS – FINE ARTS

A joke is an epigram on the death of a feeling.

U Mass – Machmer Hall

70

*IF THIS BE FREEDOM IN ITS FINEST FORM, THEN IT IS
ALSO FREEDOM IN ITS FINAL HOUR.*

PRINCETON – GREEN HALL

**IT'S NOT THE PRICE YOU PAY, OR THE LIFE YOU WASTE,
IT'S THE CHANCE YOU TOOK.**

COLUMBIA

Who needs help if no one knows it?

Radcliffe/Harvard – Lehman Hall

EVERYONE IS OBSERVANT, BUT EACH SEES THINGS
OUR OWN WAY.

URI – LIBRARY

Normality distorts reality.

Yale – Dunbam Lab

*TUESDAY IS THE WEDNESDAY OF THE REST OF YOUR
LIFE.*

PRINCETON – GUYOT HALL

**IT'S ALWAYS DARKEST JUST BEFORE THE LIGHTS GO
OUT.**

***COLUMBIA – SCHERMERHORN
HALL***

Cornell – Rockefeller Hall

Detours are sometimes taken from the serious road to achievement.

QUESTION: WHY DID FREUD CROSS THE ROAD?
ANSWER: WHEN DID YOU FIRST NOTICE THIS
INTEREST IN ROADS?

PRINCETON – GREEN HALL

Question: What do you get when you cross a donkey with an onion?

Answer: A piece of ass that will bring tears to your eyes.

U Mass – Student Union

QUESTION: WHAT DO YOU GET WHEN YOU CROSS AN OWL WITH A ROOSTER?
ANSWER: A COCK THAT STAYS UP ALL NIGHT.

RADCLIFFE/HARVARD –
LEHMAN HALL

QUESTION: WHAT IS GREEN AND COMES IN BROWNIES?
ANSWER: BOY SCOUTS.

U MASS – GOODELL LIBRARY

With my luck, when my ship finally comes in I'll be at the airport.

NYU – Loeb Student Center

"PEEL THAT CORN," HE SAID, HUSKILY. "I HATE THE STRINGS," SHE SAID, SILKENLY.

CORNELL – CLARK SCIENCE
CENTER

Question: If the stork brings white babies, and the raven brings black babies, who brings no babies?
Answer: The swallow.

SUNY Albany – Library

YOUR SISTER IS LIKE A BOWLING BOWL—SHE GETS PICKED UP, FINGERED, THROWN IN THE GUTTER AND COMES BACK FOR MORE.

U MASS – MACHMER

**A LITTLE BIRD WITH A YELLOW BILL
SAT UPON MY WINDOW SILL.
I COAXED IT IN WITH BITS OF BREAD,
AND THEN I SMASHED ITS FUCKIN' HEAD.**

BOSTON U – HAYDEN HALL

Did you hear about the two gay judges who tried each other?

Brown – Barus/Halley

QUESTION: WHAT DO YOU CALL A MOUNTAIN
CLIMBER WITH A VASECTOMY?
ANSWER: DRY SACK ON THE ROCKS.

*BOSTON COLLEGE – MCGUINN
HALL*

When Kojak dreams he has Tellie visions.

NYU – Meyer Hall

*DID YOU HEAR ABOUT THE CRAB WHO HAD
INSOMNIA? HE COULD ONLY SLEEP IN SNATCHES.*

NYU – BARNEY BUILDING

**ALL KNOWLEDGE AVAILABLE TO MANKIND HAS BEEN
MICROFILMED AND CLEVERLY STORED ON THE TONGUE OF
HOWARD COSELL.**

CCNY – MOTT HALL

Incest is relative.

CCNY – Curry Hall

74

CELIBACY IS HEREDITARY.

NYU – BIOLOGY

I've had a belly full of onphaloskepsis!

NYU – Bobst Library

SPELLING IS A LOSSED ART.

U MASS – FINE ARTS

VACUUM SUCKS!

PRINCETON – FINE HALL

Space is a vacuum because Earth sucks.

Boston College – McGuinn Hall

DIARRHEA IS HEREDITARY; IT RUNS IN YOUR GENES.

BOSTON U – HAYDEN HALL

Hamilton Jordan and Jimmy Carter: coke and a smile.

Temple – Student Activities Center

JERRY FORD THINKS VETO POWERS IS AN ITALIAN SPY PILOT.

SUNY ALBANY – LIBRARY

ITALIAN WEDDING INVITATION: U, 2, D, WEDDING, ROSA, MR.

PENN – BENNET HALL

Question: What are the five worst years in an Italian's life?
Answer: 3rd grade.

U Mass – Student Union

QUESTION: WHAT DO YOU CALL THE ITALIAN NAVY?
ANSWER: CHICKENS OF THE SEA.

PENN – BENNET HALL

Question: Why would Pollacks make terrible parachutists?
Answer: They would miss the ground.

Temple – Curtis Hall

QUESTION: WHAT DO YOU CALL A POLLACK WHO MARRIES A GORILLA?
ANSWER: A SOCIAL CLIMBER.

PENN – WILLIAMS HALL

QUESTION: WHAT DOES THE BOTTOM OF A POLISH SODA BOTTLE SAY?
ANSWER: OPEN OTHER END.

TEMPLE – CURTIS HALL

Time flies like an arrow.
Fruit flies like a banana.
Horse flies like a Pollack.

Brown – Lincoln Field Building

DID YOU HEAR ABOUT THE POLISH GIRL WHO
WANTED TO TRADE IN HER MENSTRUAL CYCLE FOR A
HONDA?

*TEMPLE – STUDENT ACTIVITIES
CENTER*

**Question: Why don't Puerto Ricans have check books?
Answer: It's too hard to sign checks with a spray can.**

Temple – Student Activities Center

*FORMULA JOKE CORNER:
QUESTION: HOW MANY LIGHTBULBS DOES IT TAKE TO
SCREW JACK'S HEAD ON STRAIGHT?
ANSWER: WHEN IT'S AJAR.*

– BELOW –

*THIS IS A TASTELESS, TACTLESS, WORTHLESS,
HUMORLESS, AND PRICELESS JOKE. I WOULD LIKE TO STATE
IRREVOCABLY THAT I HAD VIRTUALLY NOTHING TO DO
WITH IT.*

– BELOW –

YOU DIDN'T. I DID. SO THERE!

HARVARD – BIOLOGICAL LABS

QUESTION: WHAT DO YOU CALL AN AUTOMATIC CAN-OPENER?

ANSWER: BIONIC PROCTOLOGIST.

HARVARD – BIOLOGICAL LABS

Question: What's better than roses on the piano?

Answer: Tulips on the organ.

Temple – Beury Hall

QUESTION: WHAT'S WORSE THAN A DEAD SKUNK ON YOUR PIANO?

ANSWER: A DISEASED BEAVER ON YOUR ORGAN.

PRINCETON – GUYOT HALL

Question: What do soybeans and vibrators have in common?

Answer: They're both meat substitutes.

Temple – Paley Library

ELLA FITZGERALD + DARTH VADER = ELLA VADER

BOSTON COLLEGE – MCGUINN HALL

$$S \frac{1}{CABIN} D(CABIN) = LOG_e\ CABIN + C = HOUSEBOAT$$

PENN – RITTENBERG LAB

Question: What's brown and sounds like a bell?

Answer: Dung.

Dartmouth – Wilder Hall

QUESTION: WHAT'S RED AND SOUNDS LIKE A BELL?
ANSWER: MAO TSE DUNG.

DARTMOUTH – WILDER HALL

Question: What do you get when you have a bunch of rabbits standing in line and they all take a step backwards at the same time?
Answer: A receding hare line.

– below –

A lot of baby rabbits.

U Mass – Student Union

QUESTION: HOW DO YOU MAKE A VENETIAN BLIND?
ANSWER: POKE HIM IN THE EYE.

PENN – WHARTON

QUESTION: HOW DO YOU MAKE A HORMONE?
ANSWER: DON'T PAY HER.

PENN – WHARTON

Question: How do you tell a boy chromosome from a girl chromosome?
Answer: Pull down its genes.

Penn – Wharton

NEW TOY! 'SUCKERMAN'! THEY SAY HE COMES IN THREE COLORS, BUT I FIND THAT HARD TO SWALLOW.

PENN – DIETRICH LIBRARY

Question: What do you call couples who practice coitus interruptus?
Answer: Parents.

Yale – Law

IT'S BETTER TO BE PISSED OFF THAN TO BE PISSED ON.
U MASS – ENGINEERING EAST

QUESTION: WHAT DO ANTS USE TO GET HIGH?
ANSWER: ANTACID.

PRINCETON – FINE HALL

Here's to the bull who roams the wood
and makes the cows all feel good.
If it weren't for him and his mighty rod,
what would we do for beef, by God?

Penn – Dietrich Library

IN DAYS OF OLDE WHEN KNIGHTS WERE BOLD
AND RUBBERS WEREN'T INVENTED,
THEY LAID A SOCK ACROSS THEIR COCK,
AND BABIES WERE PREVENTED.

BROWN – BARUS/HALLEY HALL

Jesus walked into the square one day and came upon a crowd that was about to stone a woman. When Jesus asked what she had done, the crowd responded that she had committed adultery. Jesus stood on a large rock and told the crowd, "Let those among you who have never sinned cast the first stone."

After a period of time a little old lady emerged from the crowd, picked up a good-sized rock and hurled it at the adultress.

Jesus turned and eyed the woman. With a disgusted look, he said, "Mom, sometimes you are a pain in the ass."

Princeton – Fine Hall

QUESTION: WHAT'S THE DIFFERENCE BETWEEN A PICK-POCKET AND A PEEPING TOM?
ANSWER: ONE SNATCHES WATCHES.

PRINCETON – FINE HALL

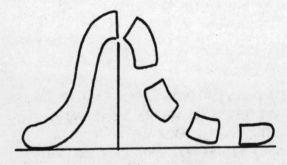

(WORM CROSSING RAZOR)

PRINCETON – FINE HALL

If you ever feel like you're up a creek without a paddle, you probably oar.

U Mass – Morrill Hall

THE ARMY CORPS OF ENGINEERS HAS SHOWN
CONCRETE PROGRESS.

– BELOW –

· THE CORPS GIVES A DAM!

PRINCETON – BEGGS HALL

**I finally got my shit together, and then somebody flushed
it.**

URI – Memorial Union

*BY SEWER I LIVED.
BY SEWER I DIED.
SOME SAY IT WAS MURDER,
BUT IT WAS SEWERCIDE.*

BROWN – METCALF LAB

**THERE ONCE WAS A GIRL FROM BEDFORD, MASS
WHO WENT INTO THE WATER UP TO HER KNEES . . .
(YOU SAY IT DOESN'T RHYME? IT WILL WHEN THE TIDE
COMES IN.)**

PRINCETON – BEGGS HALL

A 20-mule team in the White House garage!

Cornell – Rockefeller Hall

Politics is one area in which graduates from Northeast schools abound. Even as students they display a mature understanding of its serious nature.

UNCLE BOZO GOES TO WASHINGTON, AND ALL HIS NEPHEWS GO TO CANADA.

SUNY ALBANY – BUSINESS
ADMINISTRATION

Reagan is okay by me. We'll see what you say in four years.

SUNY Albany – Library

UNDER REAGAN, AMERICA WILL ONCE AGAIN BECOME AN IMPREGNABLE FORTRESS.

– BELOW –

DOES THAT MEAN THERE WILL BE FEWER BABIES?
COLUMBIA – URIS HALL

ANDERSON FOR PRESIDENT.

– BELOW –

BETTER LUCK NEXT TIME.
PENN – WHARTON

LBJ went all the way.

Temple – Annenberg Hall

CARTER IN '84.

– BELOW –

GOOD JOKE!

– BELOW –

WHO CARES?

U MASS – GOODELL LIBRARY

Kennedy in 1984: If you don't support him you are the loser.

– below –

If you do support him you're the loser. We'll be a welfare state, if we aren't already.

U Mass – Goodell Library

SUPPORT THE REVOLUTION! REMOVE REAGAN IN THE 80's.

– BELOW –

. . . AND ELECT NIXON, YOU LILY WHITE BLEEDING HEART LIBERALS.

U MASS – GOODELL LIBRARY

QUESTION: WHAT LAYS BEHIND EVERY WATERGATE? ANSWER: A MILHOUS.

YALE – BECTON CENTER

The Moral Majority is neither.

Princeton – Guyot Hall

LET'S HEAR IT FOR THE IMMORAL MAJORITY.

COLUMBIA

Be American! Join a fundamentalist church and lower your IQ score by 30 to 40 points.

Columbia

NUKE A REPUBLICAN TODAY!

> *BOSTON U – STONE SCIENCE*
> *BUILDING*

NUKE THE WORLD A BETTER PLACE TO LIVE.

> ***SUNY ALBANY – HUMANITIES***

Nuke me all over baby.
Ooo-weee!
Nuke me all night long.

> *Dartmouth – Wilder Hall*

MOTHER, DO YOU THINK THEY'LL DROP THE
BOMB?

> *TEMPLE – ANNENBERG HALL*

Love the bomb!

> ***Penn – Moore Electrical***
> ***Engineering***

PLEASE HELP STOP NUKES, THEY WILL KILL US.

> *RADCLIFFE/HARVARD –*
> *LEHMAN HALL*

MORE NUKES, LESS KOOKS!

> ***REST AREA ON HWY 89, NORTH***
> ***OF BOSTON***

Seabrook, May 24.

Brown – Psychology

MUTANTS FOR NUKES!

BOSTON U – STONE SCIENCE
BUILDING

More people have died in Ted Kennedy's car than in nuclear power plants.

U Mass – Marston Hall

(STICKER) *NUCLEAR FACT #31: MORE THAN 1 OUT OF 4 URANIUM MINERS DIE OF LUNG CANCER FROM RADON GAS.*

– BELOW –

FACT: YOUR TAX MONEY GOES TO PAY OVER ONE BILLION BUCKS A YEAR TO COAL MINERS WHO HAVE CONTRACTED BLACK LUNG DISEASE.

– BELOW –

POWER KILLS!

RADCLIFFE/HARVARD – SCIENCE
CENTER

SOLAR POWER!

PENN – WILLIAMS HALL

Ban the use of solar power! Conserve the sun!

Yale – Osborn Lab

BLOOD IS THICKER THAN OIL. RESIST THE DRAFT!

YALE – LEET OLIVER HALL

Insist that the resistors who persist in resisting do desist from persisting in insisting that resisters continue in resisting the draft.

Yale – Law

I AM AN AMERICAN IMPERIALIST AND PROUD OF IT. LONG LIVE THE MANIFEST DESTINY!

PENN – MOORE ELECTRICAL
ENGINEERING

JOIN THE ARMY. TRAVEL TO EXOTIC LANDS. MEET INTERESTING FOREIGN PEOPLE. KILL THEM.

PRINCETON – AGRICULTURE

War is murder for profit.

– below –

. . . and fun.

– below –

What murder isn't for profit?

– below –

What profit isn't for fun?

Harvard – Sever Hall

WAR DOESN'T PROVE WHO IS RIGHT, ONLY WHO IS LEFT.

TEMPLE – BEURY HALL

There is a bad force.

– below –

Force is always bad.

U Mass – Fine Arts

IMPEACH CAPITALISM!

YALE – LAW

DEATH TO COMMIS!

– BELOW –

DEATH TO CAPITALISTS WHO CAN'T SPELL!

PENN – WILLIAMS HALL

Free Eastern Europe from the neo-colonialist Russian oppressors!

SUNY Albany – Social Science

DON'T TRUST THE ROOSKIES!

HARVARD – BIOLOGICAL LABS

You'd think it unfortunate enough that the Soviet Union has given Socialism a bad name, without insisting on continuing under that name.

SUNY Albany – Library

WORKERS OF THE WORLD, DISPERSE!

TEMPLE – CURTIS HALL

FUCK THE IRANIANS! DRILL DOWN UNDER THEM AND SUCK THE OIL FROM UNDER THEM.

HARVARD – BIOLOGICAL LABS

May a herd of frenzied camels run over the next Iranian who opens his mouth in protest.

Harvard – Emerson Hall

DEPORT ALL IRANIAN STUDENTS TO ITALY.

BROWN – BARUS/HALLEY HALL

90

Sticks and stones may break my bones, but I still got your money. —The Shah.

– below –

The sticks and stones got him.

Yale – Becton Center

LET'S LEAVE THE POLITICAL COMMENTS OFF THIS WALL AND LEAVE THEM IN THE TOILET WHERE THEY BELONG.

SUNY ALBANY – LIBRARY

WHAT'S WITH ALL THIS POLITICAL CRAP? WHAT HAPPENED TO GOOD OLD-FASHIONED SMUT?

TEMPLE – PALEY LIBRARY

Fuck shit!

Penn – Dietrich Library

HARVARD – SCIENCE CENTER

Among all issues deemed important by politically minded students from the Northeast, none can match the universality of the whale.

Take a whale to lunch!

Amberst – Frost Library

DO YOU KNOW WHERE YOUR WHALES ARE TONIGHT?

BROWN – METCALF LIBRARY

DO WHALES HAVE PUBIC HAIR?

PRINCETON – GUYOT HALL

Nuke the whales!

– below –

Whale the nukes!

Penn – Moore Electrical Engineering

NUKE THE GAY WHALES IN LOVE CANAL!

BROWN – BARUS/HALLEY HALL

Nuke the whalers!

Penn – Dietrich Library

SAVE THE WHALES!
TRADE THEM WITH YOUR FRIENDS.

HARVARD – BIOLOGICAL LABS

CLONE THE WHALES!

HARVARD – BIOLOGICAL LABS

Drop the whale on Iran!

U Mass – Thompson

DROP THE WHALE ON IVAN!

U MASS – GOODELL LIBRARY

Draft the whales; save them from a monotonous life at sea.

Harvard – Biological Labs

You can trust graffiti...

... Rockefellers don't write any.

BROWN – METCALF LAB

As successful graduates, students from the Northeast will be expected to have mastered the office memo, the business letter, and the legal brief. This, perhaps, explains the high regard in which graffiti are held.

Why is there no intelligent, pungently witty graffiti in a bathroom occupied by such supposedly eloquent bullshit artists as Yale Law School students?

– below –

Because all the eloquent bullshit is in the Yale Law Review.

Yale – Law

ACTUALLY, THE GRAFFITI AT THIS BASTION OF IVY IS QUITE WEAK, UNDOUBTEDLY A REFLECTION OF THE STUDENT BODY'S FRUSTRATION OVER BEING REJECTED FROM HARVARD. (RAH! RAH! RAH!) PLEASE PROVE ME WRONG. THESE SPACIOUS WALLS ARE JUST WAITING TO RECEIVE YOUR PEARLS OF WIT AND WISDOM. LET 'EM RIP! —A VISITOR.

DARTMOUTH – WILDER HALL

You are what you eat—shit.

– below –

We appear to have been infiltrated by someone who does not understand the nature of *class* graffiti.

Harvard – Biological Labs

GRAND PRIZE – PRINCETON GRAFFITI AWARD.

PRINCETON – WOOLWORTH CENTER

HAVE YOU NOTICED THE LACK OF GOOD SCATALOGICAL GRAFFITI AT YALE?

YALE – WOOLSEY HALL

Good graffiti is as important to education as an all-college meeting.

Amherst – Frost Library

AND NOW THAT THE ICE HAS BROKEN, THE GRAFFITI MADNESS MAY ONCE AGAIN COMMENCE.

PRINCETON – BRACKETT HALL

Why is there no graffiti here? Don't teachers own pens?

Yale – Graduate School

WRITE ON!

PENN – RITTENBERG LAB

THIS CONCRETE SURE IN HELL NEEDS HUMANIZING.

U MASS – FINE ARTS

Write on walls.
Stall walls.
All walls.
Even tall mall walls.

Boston U – Hayden Hall

I CAN READ THE WRITING ON THE WALL.

PENN – WILLIAMS HALL

There is drama on these walls.

CCNY – Cohen Library

Graffiti are FUN!

U MASS – MACHMER HALL

GRAFFITI IS OUR MIND'S WAY OF FARTING.

YALE – GRADUATE SCHOOL

All graffiti is misspelled.

Yale – Dunham Lab

CONSTIPATION BREEDS GRAFFITI.

CORNELL – PLANT SCIENCES

Graffiti are the people's mailman.

Yale – Sterling Library

(ON HALLWAY DOOR)
SKI CLUB PEOPLE! THANK YOU! SIGNED, THE HALL SWEEPER.

U MASS – UNION

(ON OFFICE DOOR)
YOU PEOPLE ALWAYS LEAVE YOUR LIGHTS ON. AREN'T YOU SUPPOSED TO BE SAVING MONEY?

U MASS – UNION

This is your conscience—please return my watch.

U Mass – Fine Arts

Leeroy, How dare you!
😠 (Just kidding) 😊

Brow

Brow — This is the only
sane carrel in
the 'brary.

LiRoy.

AMHERST – FROST LIBRARY

Es wird etwas geschehen.

– below –

Fuckin' kraut!

Penn – Williams Hall

THIS DOOR IS IN ITS 4TH PRINTING.

PENN – DIETRICH LIBRARY

THEY OUGHT TO GET SOME LIGHT IN HERE SO THE WRITING ON THIS WALL CAN BE READ! —A STUDENT CONCERNED ABOUT THE ILLITERACY PROBLEM.

BOSTON U – LAW AUDITORIUM

This side for graffiti for posterity. The other side for graffiti for passing.

Harvard – Pierce Hall

CONSIDERATE GRAFFITI VANDALS USE PENCILS.

– BELOW –

REFLECTIVE VANDALS USE MIRRORS.

– BELOW –

SECRETIVE VANDALS USE INVISIBLE INK.

– BELOW –

KINKY VANDALS USE LEATHER.

– BELOW –

COOL VANDALS USE DRUGS.

– BELOW –

HORNY VANDALS USE EACH OTHER.

PRINCETON – BEGGS HALL

Med School has better graffiti.

Boston U – Law Building

BIOLOGISTS DON'T HAVE TIME FOR GRAFFITI.

CORNELL – STIMSON HALL

THE WRITTEN WORD IS A COMMITMENT, SO AT LEAST BE CONSCIOUS OF WHAT YOU WRITE.

SUNY ALBANY – LIBRARY

Theatrical people are of above average I.Q., so let's show some imagination in graffiti.

Temple – Annenberg Hall

IF I HAD KNOWN HOW BORING THIS WALL WAS GOING TO BE, I WOULD HAVE GONE SOMEWHERE ELSE.

PENN – DIETRICH LIBRARY

Why don't women write things on their bathroom walls? I'm tired of this B.S. about lesbians and schools. Let's have some good dirty jokes and comments.

CCNY – Shepard Hall

I'M TIRED OF READING ALL THIS TRASHY GRAFFITI. THIS IS WHAT WOMEN'S LIB IS ALL ABOUT?

– BELOW –

NO, THIS IS KNOWN AS FIRST YEAR ADOLESCENT FEMINISM.

– BELOW –

THIS IS KNOWN AS BULLSHIT.

– BELOW –

OH, SHUT UP!

– BELOW –

PUERILE INABILITY TO CONFRONT DIFFERING OPINIONS.

> *RADCLIFFE/HARVARD –*
> *LEHMAN HALL*

PISS IN THE URINAL AND THIS SHIT ON THE WALL.

> ***DARTMOUTH – WILDER HALL***

If all the negative graffiti were channeled into one source, we could probably run the world with all the power and solve the energy problem with the bullshit.

> *Amherst – Frost Library*

WHY DON'T YOU PROTEST INSTEAD OF WRITING ON BATHROOM WALLS.

> *SUNY ALBANY – LIBRARY*

STAMP OUT GRAFFITI!!!

Cornell – Franklin Hall

BAN GRAFFITI!

BROWN – MARSTON HALL

IF IT WEREN'T FOR GRAFFITI, THEY WOULDN'T WASH THE BATHROOM WALLS AS OFTEN.

AMHERST – FROST LIBRARY

To think that the University pays someone to halt this dissemination of knowledge.

Princeton – Fine Hall

(NEAR ERASURE)
THE JACKBOOT OF THE IMPERIALIST OPPRESSOR IS ONCE AGAIN AT THE NECK OF THE GRAFFITI PROLETARIAT.

HARVARD – BIOLOGICAL LABS

Nuclear power means cancer, mutations, and death!

But it has
its drawbacks too.
Yale – Law

One sign of their preparation for success: students in the Northeast want to have the last word. Many graffiti fall victim to a well-chosen retort.

JESUS SAVES!

– BELOW –

SO CAN YOU, AT WOOLWORTH'S.

PRINCETON – McCOSH HALL

FOR A CHALLENGING CAREER, JOIN THE NAZI ORGANIZATION IN THE U.S.

– BELOW –

FOR A SOMEWHAT MORE CHALLENGING CAREER, JOIN THE NAZI ORGANIZATION IN ISRAEL.

PENN – DIETRICH LIBRARY

Kill all non-appreciatives!

– below –

I can appreciate that.

U Mass – Bartlett Hall

PLEASE DON'T RUN AMUCK.

– BELOW –

TRUE, MUCKS TIRE EASILY AND SHOULD ONLY BE WALKED.

NYU – LOEB STUDENT CENTER

Jesus saves!

– below –

Esposito scores on rebounds.

Classic on all campuses

YOU CAN'T GET TO THE 4TH FLOOR THIS WAY.

– BELOW –

ISN'T IT ALWAYS A ROUND ABOUT WAY TO THE TOP.

U MASS – FINE ARTS

BULLSHIT!

– BELOW –

CEASE THE BOVINE SCATALOGY.

DARTMOUTH – STEELE HALL

I love Annie!

– below –

We do too!

U Mass – Student Union

ALL THAT IS GOLD DOES NOT GLITTER.
NOT ALL THOSE WHO WANDER ARE LOST.

– BELOW –

BUT WE ARE TALKING ABOUT 95% CONFIDENCE
INTERVALS!

PENN – WHARTON

(On an otherwise blank right-hand stall wall)
Where are all the left-handers?

– below –

They're certainly not with the Red Sox.

Harvard – Biological Labs

STOP THE WORLD, I WANT TO GET OFF.

– BELOW –

GETTING OFF IS YOUR OWN RESPONSIBILITY.
                                    PRINCETON – GREEN HALL

YOU CAN PICK YOUR NOSE, BUT YOU CAN'T PICK YOUR FRIENDS.

– BELOW –

BUT YOU CAN PICK YOUR FRIEND'S NOSE.
                                    SUNY ALBANY – LEARNING
                                    CENTER

Fight the draft!

– below –

Apply weather-stripping.
                                    Dartmouth – Steele Hall

WHAT DOES "IT" MEAN IN THE SENTENCE, "WHAT TIME IS IT?"

– BELOW –

WHAT'S IT TO YOU?
                                    BOSTON U – HAYDEN HALL

Often the retort becomes a series of responses.

Free Sacco and Vanzetti!

– below –

I'll take a pair.

– below –

A pair of Rosenbergs wins.

Amberst – Frost Library

WE ARE ALL VIET CONG.

– BELOW –

EXCEPT MY MOM.

– BELOW –

TYPICAL LEFTIST INDIVIDUALISM.

HARVARD – EMERSON HALL

I LIKE GRILS!

– BELOW –

THAT'S 'GIRLS', YOU IDIOT!

– BELOW –

WHAT ABOUT US 'GRILS'?

HARVARD – JEFFERSON HALL

"Dry ox tail in rear" —Make one word from these letters.

– below –

Dryoxtailinrear.

– below –

Extraordinarily.

Penn – Rittenberg Lab

BURGER KING IS A CAPITALIST INSTITUTION.

– BELOW –

COME TO THINK OF IT, MARXISTS NEVER COULD MAKE GOOD HAMBURGER.

– BELOW –

THAT'S TRUE. HOWEVER, LET US NOT FORGET THE FRANKFURTER SCHOOL.

– BELOW –

REVISIONIST HOT DOGS!

CORNELL – MCGRAW HALL

And then series become longer.

Phamous Phils:

– below –

Phil Harmonic

– below –

Phil Anthropist

– below –

Phil Osopher

– below –

Phil Ees

– below –

Phil Thee

Temple – Paley Library

THE WORLD OUT THERE IS A JUNGLE.

– BELOW –

NO, IT'S NOT! YOU'RE LION!

– BELOW –

LET'S HAVE SOME SERIOUS GRAFFITI. STOP MONKEYING AROUND.

– BELOW –

UNFOUNDED ALLIGATORTIONS!

– BELOW –

THAT'S A CROC!

– BELOW –

BE CREATIVE! WRITE SOMETHING GNU!
DARTMOUTH – BAKER HALL

DON'T YOU HAVE SOMETHING BETTER TO DO THAN WRITE ON WALLS?

– BELOW –

AND YOURSELF?

– BELOW –

WHO ARE YOU REFERRING TO?

– BELOW –

YOU!

– BELOW –

110

THEN WHAT ABOUT YOU?

– BELOW –

WHO? ME?

– BELOW –

YOU!

– BELOW –

I'M AN EXCEPTION.

AMHERST – FROST LIBRARY

Gag—Ha! Ha!
    Ha! Ha!

– below –

Wog—What?
    What?

– below –

Fog—(cloud)
    (cloud)

– below –

Log—Chop!
    Chop!

– below –

Frog—Rivet!
     Rivet!

– below –

Dog—Arf!
     Arf!

– below –

Whiz—Fizz!
     Fizz!

– below –

Tog—Clomp!
     Clomp!

– below –

Pig—Oink!
     Oink!

– below –

Gag—mpfh
     mpfh

– below –

Fag—Swish.
     Swish.

– below –

112

Sag—Bounce
    Bounce

– below –

Lag—Frump.
    Frump.

Brown – Lincoln Field Building

DEFINE:
ISOTHERM—BECAUSE I EXERTHIZE
ISOTOPE—WHAT AN IDIOT I AM
ISOBAR—ITALIAN DRINKING PLACE

– BELOW –

ISOTONE—BECAUSE I LAY IN THE SUN

– BELOW –

ICICLE—

(eye cycle)

– BELOW –

ICECREAM—I SCREAM, YOU SCREAM, WE ALL SCREAM
FOR ICE CREAM.

– BELOW –

I'S IN TROUBLE

– BELOW –

ICE MAN COMETH

– BELOW –

I S'POSE

– BELOW –

I SEE

– BELOW –

ICY

– BELOW –

ICBM

– BELOW –

I SEEK SHELTER

– BELOW –

I SEE B.M.

– BELOW –

I'SE SO HAPPY

– BELOW –

ISOP'S FABLES.

YALE – DUNHAM LAB

I don't like to write papers.

– below –

You're not alone.

– below –

I agree with you.

– below –

Neither do I.

– below –

Me neither.

– below –

Likewise.

– below –

Nor I.

– below –

Same here.

– below –

No doubt about it.

– below –

Definitely.

– below –

For sure.

– below –

Unmistakably.

– below –

No shit.

– below –

You can say that again.

– below –

A-yep, yep, yep. A huh-huh. A-yep.

– below –

Papers do suck, without a doubt.

Amberst – Frost Library

116

BASIC SELMODYNAMICS!

– BELOW –

*NO, ELMODYNAMICS—THE STUDY OF ELMO
TRANSFERS.*

– BELOW –

*DO YOU KNOW WHAT THE 1ST LAW OF
ELMODYNAMICS IS?*

– BELOW –

*FOR EVERY ELMO THERE IS AN EQUAL AND OPPOSITE
RE-ELMO.*

– BELOW –

*THE SCIENCE OF ELMO WAS FOUNDED BY ELMO P.
FUDD, BUT MANY OF ITS MOST IMPRESSIVE ACHIEVEMENTS
HAVE BEEN MADE BY SEVERAL PRINCETON PROFESSORS.*

– BELOW –

AND WHAT IS AN ELMOTROPIC PROCESS?

– BELOW –

IS THAT WHAT THEY DO AT THE PLASMA-ELMO LAB?

– BELOW –

NO, AN ELMOTROPIC IS WHERE ELMOS GO FOR VACATION.

– BELOW –

TELL ME ABOUT THE IDEAL ELMO LAW.

– BELOW –

IT'S ELMOMENTORY, MY DEAR DR. WATSON.

– BELOW –

OBVIOUSLY FOR ELMORONS.

PRINCETON – BRACKET HALL

Speaking of limericks,
Did you ever notice
That 'God' and 'dog'
Don't rhyme?

CORNELL – MCGRAW HALL

No one is ready to master the world who has not mastered the limerick.

There is a young man in McGraw
whose dong can inspire awe.
It's not only its size
that will open your eyes,
but the fact that it's shaped like a claw.

Cornell – McGraw Hall

THERE ONCE WAS A FELLOW NAMED DAVE
WHO DUG UP A WHORE FROM A GRAVE.
SHE WAS MOLDY AS SHIT
AND WAS MISSING A TIT,
BUT THINK OF THE MONEY HE SAVED.

CLASSIC ON ALL CAMPUSES

There once was a girl from West Hemes
who was plagued with excessive wet dreams.
She saved up a dozen
and sent to her cousin,
who ate them as if they were creams.

Boston College – Fulton Hall

AN AMERICAN CAUGHT IN TEHRAN
SAID, "I WISH I'D BEEN SENT TO CEYLON."
"THAT COLONIAL NAME,"
SAID KHOMEINI, " 'S PROFANE,
UNGODLY IMPERIALIST PAWN."

HARVARD – BIOLOGICAL LABS

THERE ONCE WAS A PHYSICIST NAMED BRECK
WHOSE ORGAN WAS SELDOM ERECT.
WHEN HIS WIFE HEARD HIM HUMMING
SHE KNEW HE WAS COMING
BECAUSE OF THE DOPPLER EFFECT.

HARVARD – JEFFERSON HALL

There was a young man named Skinner
who took his girlfriend to dinner.
At a quarter to nine
they sat down to dine,
and at quarter to ten he was in her.

Temple – Curtis Hall

THERE ONCE WAS A FELLOW NAMED HOWARD
WHOSE PENIS WAS NUCLEAR-POWERED.
WHILE GRABBIN' SOME ASS,
HE REACHED CRITICAL MASS.
(JUST THINK OF THE GIRL HE DEFLOWERED.)

PENN – WILLIAMS HALL

**There was a young girl name Helene
whose features were frightfully plain.
But for painters of merit
she was happy to bear it
for the thrill of appearing 'en peint'.**

Princeton – McCormick Hall

*THERE ONCE WAS A MAN FROM MCBRIDE
WHO FELL IN A SHIT HOLE AND DIED.
HIS OVERCOME BROTHER
FELL INTO THE OTHER,
AND NOW THEY'RE INTERRED SIDE BY SIDE.*

PRINCETON – STUDENT CENTER

HARVARD DIPLOMAS— TAKE ONE

CLASSIC ON ALL EASTERN
CAMPUSES

So eager are the Northeast's students to hone their writing skills that they will use any excuse to ink their thoughts. A favorite excuse is the toilet-paper dispenser.

Brown diplomas, insert $40,000.00

Brown – Metcalf Lab

DIPLOMAS FROM THE JAMES EARL CARTER 'LEARN
WHILE YOU EARN' SCHOOL OF PRESIDENCY

U MASS – BARTLETT HALL

TOILET LEAVES.

SUNY ALBANY – CHEMISTRY

Sacramental wipe for Holy Shit.

SUNY Albany – Social Science

(OVER ADJACENT   *(OVER THIRD, EMPTY*
DISPENSERS)   *DISPENSER)*

REGULAR   UNLEADED   HIGH TEST
(SOLD OUT)

SUNY ALBANY – PHYSICS

Other items of the toilet inspire as well.

(on a paper-towel dispenser)
Princeton condoms—cover organ and secure with rubber band.

Princeton – Palmer Hall

SIGN ON TOWEL DISPENSER: "ONE TOWEL DRIES BOTH HANDS."

(Beneath sign)

WHAT IS THE SOUND OF ONE HAND DRYING?

– BELOW –

FOR $10,000 PER YEAR, I'LL TAKE TWO, THANK YOU.
PENN – DIETRICH LIBRARY

(ON PROPHYLACTIC DISPENSER IN WOMEN'S ROOM)
DON'T BUY THESE, SLEEP WITH A FRIEND.

– BELOW –

AIN'T NOTHING LIKE THE REAL THING.

– BELOW –

DON'T BUY THIS GUM. IT TASTES LIKE RUBBER.
U MASS – CAMPUS CENTER

(arrow to stall latch)
John Locke

Harvard – Emerson Hall

(ON HOT-AIR HAND DRYER)
FOR THE LATEST FROM KHOMEINI, PRESS.
U MASS – STUDENT UNION

(in center of brick wall)
Just another brick in the wall.

Princeton – Palmer Hall

(ON BLANK WALL)
HELP STAMP OUT THIS KIND OF THINKING!
PENN – WILLIAMS HALL

(NEXT TO HOLE IN WALL)
I'M PEEKING AT YOU.

*BOSTON COLLEGE – FULTON
HALL*

(On brick wall in men's room)
So, this is a brick shithouse!

Princeton – Student Center

(IN RED)
RED INK WRITES!

SUNY ALBANY – FINE ARTS

(next to picture of a limp penis)
Portrait of the artist as an old man.

Yale – Law

(BACKWARDS ON OUTSIDE GLAZED WINDOW)
HELLO WORLD!

SUNY ALBANY – FINE ARTS

(BOTTOM OF STALL DOOR)
BEWARE OF LIMBO DANCERS!

U MASS – MACHMER HALL

(on wall behind stool)
Don't break your neck!

Harvard – Pierce Hall

(WRITTEN ON GROUT BETWEEN NUMEROUS ADJACENT TILES)

NOBODY CARES, IF YOU WRITE BETWEEN SQUARES.

IT TAKES GREAT ZEAL, TO WRITE IN A SEAL.

IT'S ALWAYS FASTER, TO WRITE ON PLASTER.

YOU MUST REALLY BE NUTTY TO WRITE ON PUTTY.

YOU INCREDIBLE LOUT, YOU'RE WRITING ON GROUT.

IT ISN'T VILE TO WRITE BETWEEN TILE.

WANT TO WRITE? USE THE WHITE.

IT'S CRAZY, SORTA, TO WRITE ON MORTAR.

ONE WRITES WITH TACT WHERE THE WALL IS CRACKED.

ISN'T IT GREAT TO WRITE WHERE IT'S STRAIGHT.

ONE MORE POEM AND I GO HOME.

HERE'S THE ONE, NOW I'M ALL DONE.

PRINCETON – WOOLWORTH CENTER

(next to electrical outlet)
Punch for service.

U Mass – Goodell Library

(ARROW POINTING TO MYSTERIOUS LARGE GRAY METAL DOOR AT TOP OF STAIRS)

GO AHEAD, I DARE YOU.

U MASS – FINE ARTS

(BELOW "EXIT" SIGN)
THERE IS NO EXIT BUT DEATH!

U MASS – FINE ARTS

126

(below sign saying "Students must sign in")
Murderers need not.

Yale – 51 Prospect Street

SPIDER, SPIDER, I LOVE YOU. *(THE WRITER THEN
PROCEEDED TO DRAW A MEANDERING LINE ACROSS THE
STALL WALL, APPARENTLY FOLLOWING THE TRAIL OF HIS
NEWFOUND LOVE.)*

PRINCETON – GREEN HALL

I like ʍɹıʇıuƃ udsıpǝ poʍu·

Harvard – Biological Labs

Sometimes the writers' attentions wandered beyond the immedi-
ate vicinity of the toilet.

*TENURE THE RHINOS, THEY'RE HORNY ABOUT THE BIO
LABS* (REFERRING TO THE RHINOCEROSES CARVED IN
THE STONE FAÇADE OF THE BIOLOGICAL LABS)

HARVARD – BIOLOGICAL LABS

RUTGERS – DANA LIBRARY

The thought of eventual achievements permeates the student's every activity in the Northeast.

THIS HAS TO BE THE BEST SHITHOUSE AT BOSTON COLLEGE. QUIET, YET TASTEFUL. THE KIND OF PLACE A MAN IS PROUD TO SHIT IN.

BOSTON COLLEGE – HIGGINS HALL

Welcome to one of the finest accommodations that the Bio Lab has to offer.

Harvard – Biological Labs

128

IS THIS REALLY THE CITY DESK OF THE TEMPLE
NEWS?

TEMPLE – ANNENBERG HALL

Stall #2, winner of three coveted awards!
1. **The Good Stall-keeping Prize**
2. **Dear Abbey Seal of Approval**
3. **The JLS International Grumble Competition**

Harvard – Biological Labs

BETTER TOILETS THROUGH SCIENCE.

CORNELL – GOODWIN SMITH
HALL

IF YOU LIVED HERE YOU'D BE HOME BY NOW.
HARVARD – BIOLOGICAL LABS

The immortal question: "Was Sagan here?"

Cornell – Clark Science Center

JOHN WAS HERE, BUT NOW HE'S GONE.
HE LEFT HIS NAME TO CARRY ON.
THOSE WHO KNEW HIM HAD A FIT.
THOSE WHO DIDN'T, CAME TO SHIT.

PRINCETON – MCCOSH HALL

Someone built this toilet.

Columbia – Philosophy

THESE STALLS DISCRIMINATE AGAINST
CLAUSTROPHOBICS.

DARTMOUTH – WILDER HALL

**THERE AIN'T ROOM IN THIS STALL FOR BOTH OF US.
YOU BETTER LEAVE BY SUNDOWN.**

RUTGERS – SMITH HALL

In days of olde
when knights were bold
and toilets weren't invented,
they laid their load
beside the road
and then they were contented.

Princeton – Guyot Hall

I'VE SHIT IN ENGLAND.
I'VE SHIT IN FRANCE.
BEFORE I'D SHIT HERE
I'D SHIT IN MY PANTS.

*BOSTON U – STONE SCIENCE
BUILDING*

**Unhappiness is a flooded john and a hole in your
sneakers.**

Temple – Annenberg Hall

*DON'T BOTHER TO COVER THE TOILET SEAT, THE
CRABS HERE CAN JUMP TEN FEET.*

YALE – LAW

**PLEASE DON'T THROW TOOTHPICKS IN THE TOILETS;
THOSE SMART LITTLE CRABS HAVE LEARNED TO POLEVAULT.**

PENN – BENNET HALL

Shitting is an ethical issue. I mean, it is less than 'okay' to shit on Thayer Street, which is why I come here.

Brown – Psychology

KLEPTOMANIAC—SOMEONE WHO CAN'T SIT ON THE COMMODE WITHOUT TAKING A SHIT.

PENN – DIETRICH LIBRARY

**Some come here to write some wit,
but some just come to TEKE a shit.**

Rutgers – Student Center

WHY DOESN'T ANYBODY GIVE A SHIT ANYMORE?

– BELOW –

I GAVE AT THE OFFICE.

– BELOW –

I THOUGHT THIS WAS WHERE YOU TOOK A SHIT, NOT GIVE ONE.

– BELOW –

OH, COME ON, HAVE YOU REALLY EVER SEEN ANYONE TAKE A SHIT? HOW WOULD THEY CARRY IT? IN THEIR POCKET?

BOSTON U – HAYDEN HALL

I SHIT, THEREFORE I AM.

HARVARD – BIOLOGICAL LABS

Je pisse, donc j'essui.

Columbia – Butler Library

THE ONLY TRUE GRATIFICATION IS A GOOD SHIT.

CORNELL – FRANKLIN HALL

**Here I sit broken-hearted,
tried to shit but only farted.
Yesterday I took a chance,
saved a dime but filled my pants.**

U Mass – Student Union

SHIT OR GET OFF THE POT!

SUNY ALBANY – FINE ARTS

PLEASE REMAIN SEATED UNTIL WE HAVE ARRIVED AT THE TERMINAL AND THE CAPTAIN HAS TURNED OFF THE 'SEAT BELT' SIGN.

CCNY – SHEPARD HALL

Here I sit and shit away
a meal that cost five bucks today.

NYU – Psychology

HERE I SIT ON THE POOPER
GIVING BIRTH TO ANOTHER STATE TROOPER.

CLASSIC ON ALL CAMPUSES

**Here I sit, buns a flexin'
giving birth to another Texan.**

Classic on all campuses

$E = MC^2 \ldots PLOP!$

DARTMOUTH – WILDER HALL

**PLOP, PLOP,
WHIZ, WHIZ.
OH, WHAT A RELIEF IT IS.**

CLASSIC ON ALL CAMPUSES

Plop, plop,
splash, splash.
There's toilet water
up my ass.

Princeton – Guyot Hall

FLUSH TWICE, IT'S A LONG WAY TO THE RESEARCH
LAB.

TEMPLE – BEURY HALL

Flush twice, send a Care Package to Khomeini.

URI – Kelly Hall

YOU ONLY HAVE TO FLUSH ONCE, THE CAFETERIA IS NEXT DOOR.

URI – MEMORIAL UNION

RE-CYCLE WASTE—EAT SHIT!

HARVARD – BIOLOGICAL LABS

Oh, my God! The remnants of a civilization wiped away.

Princeton – East Pyne

TIGHTEN SPHINCTER BEFORE LEAVING.

HARVARD – BIOLOGICAL LABS

To wee or not to wee ...

Brown – Barus/Halley Hall

BE LIKE POP, NOT LIKE SIS, LIFT THE LID BEFORE YOU PISS.

CLASSIC ON ALL CAMPUSES

THE FUTURE OF AMERICA IS IN YOUR HANDS.

PRINCETON – MCCOSH HALL

Why are you looking up here? The joke's in your hand.

Rutgers – Hill Hall

DON'T LOOK UP HERE, YOU ARE PISSING ON YOUR
PANT LEG.

CLASSIC ON ALL CAMPUSES

**New York City Fire Department exam: If you can piss over
the line, you pass.**

Columbia

FUCK PEPSI! THIS *IS THE PAUSE THAT REFRESHES.*

HARVARD – BIOLOGICAL LABS

**THESE ARE THE RAUNCHIEST URINALS IN THE WESTERN
HEMISPHERE.**

– BELOW –

TRY THE PISSOIRS AT THE SACRE COEUR.

*BROWN – LINCOLN FIELD
BUILDING*

Please don't eat the urinal cakes.

Yale – Osborn Labs

WASH YOUR HANDS THOROUGHLY OR PALMS WILL
GROW IN YOUR HAIR.

CORNELL – FRANKLIN HALL

Logic is the outhouse of life.

Amherst – Frost Library

There is evidence that not all students in the Northeast find rational thought a useful tool for attaining success.

WHEN THE GOING GETS WEIRD, THE WEIRD TURN PRO.

> *PRINCETON – WOOLWORTH CENTER*

QUESTION: WHAT'S WORSE THAN A FORLORN DUCLOD? ANSWER: A VAGRANT SNITZ.

> *PENN – PSYCHOLOGY*

The only good duclod is a German duclod, whether he's with his wife or his gay lover.

– below –

What's a duclod?

– below –

A treclod with a window where his other closet should be.

– below –

There are no German duclods. All humans are guzzards.

U Mass – Student Union

A DUCLOD STANDS UP FOR ITSELF IN TWO CLOSETS.

DARTMOUTH – BAKER HALL

Question: How do you put four elephants in a duclod?

– below –

Answer: Prematurely!

Temple – Curtis Hall

A SMITH & WESSON BEATS FOUR ACES.

SUNY ALBANY – FINE ARTS

QUESTION: IS IT FASTER TO NEW YORK OR BY BUS?
ANSWER: BUT WHY A DUCK?

AMHERST – FROST LIBRARY

Question: What's the difference between a rock?
Answer: The more you polish it.

Princeton – Fine Hall

QUESTION: WHAT'S THE DIFFERENCE BETWEEN A
STOVE?
ANSWER: NO, MEATBALLS DON'T BOUNCE.

AMHERST – FROST LIBRARY

Who was more moral, the Walrus or the Carpenter?

Princeton – Beggs Hall

DO NOT GO TO THE ELVES FOR COUNSEL, FOR THEY
WILL SAY BOTH 'YES' AND 'NO'.

SUNY ALBANY – FINE ARTS

IT IS NOT LIKE THE WARRIOR TO PITY HIMSELF.

PENN – BENNET HALL

Exponential catastrophe!

SUNY Albany – Library

138

pi = 3.141592653589793236<u>547173</u> ...
WRONG!
4626433827

HARVARD – JEFFERSON HALL

Have you checked for ear babies lately?

U Mass – Fine Arts

DID YOU KNOW THAT THERE IS 21.7 SQUARE MILES OF NIPPLE TISSUE IN THE US?

U MASS – MACHMER

**SHE CAME FROM PLANET CLAIRE,
I KNOW SHE CAME FROM THERE.**

PRINCETON – BRACKETT HALL

England!

Harvard – Biological Labs

ARE YOU IN YOUR OWN PRIVATE IDAHO?

RUTGERS – STUDENT CENTER

Go climb the Empire State Building!

Harvard – Emerson Hall

*THOSE WHO LIVE IN WEST L.A.
GET TO ENJOY EVERY SUNNY DAY.*

PENN – BENNET HALL

I'M AS HONEST AS A DENVER MAN CAN BE.

AMHERST – FROST LIBRARY

Hemispherical polygamy!

SUNY Albany – Library

AMALGAMATE!

CORNELL – MCGRAW HALL

Say it quiet.
Say it loud.
Say it in private.
Say it in a crowd.

Cornell – Morrill Hall

A RIVER KEEPS ON TALKING, BUT YOU NEVER HEAR A WORD IT SAYS.

U MASS – BARTLETT HALL

OH, STOP THAT, YOU'RE EXCITING ME.

YALE – STERLING LIBRARY

Santa says, "Consume while you still can."

Yale – Sterling Library

IF PIGS HAD WINGS THEY'D BE PIGEONS.

YALE – DUNHAM LAB

140

VEAL: It is radically, yet with some profound justification, considered by many residents of Kostka Second to be the most ethereal and therefore revered of all hot meals.

Think not, onlookers, that we hold these truths in a jocundly fashion. We, as our forefathers of yesterday, hold them to be extremely self-evident.

Boston College – Fulton Hall

DOGS ARE UNETHICAL BEINGS.

BROWN – PSYCHOLOGY

DO YOU WALK TO SCHOOL OR BRING YOUR LUNCH?

AMHERST – FROST LIBRARY

Bozo, the last American hero! Bozo rules!

U Mass – Goodell Library

PENN – MOORE ELECTRICAL ENGINEERING

Bring back streaking!

TEMPLE – CURTIS HALL

SQUEEZE A ZIT TODAY!

TEMPLE – ANNENBERG HALL

**COMIC COMETS
BURN BRIGHT
AT DAWN'S EDGE
SPILLING THEIR LIGHT
FOR THOSE WHO CARE.**

*URI – RESOURCE DEVELOPMENT
CENTER*

I said room!
Room service!
I'm down here on the floor!

Amherst – Frost Library

YOUR CADILLAC'S GOT A WHEEL IN THE DITCH AND
A WHEEL ON THE TRACK.

U MASS – GOODELL LIBRARY

Sartre is fartre!

Yale – Graduate School

RHOIDS FOREVER!

PRINCETON – STUDENT CENTER

FRODO LIVES!

PRINCETON – STUDENT CENTER

Buddy Holly lives!

URI – Library

COME AND SING A SIMPLE SONG.

HARVARD – EMERSON HALL

Sing for your supper and get tomatoes.

U Mass – Fine Arts

SPOOCH!

– BELOW –

FIVE FRIED SPOOCHES TO GO PLEASE.

– BELOW –

PLEASE TELL ME, WHAT'S A SPOOCH?

U MASS – GOODELL LIBRARY

ONIONS SUCK!

BROWN – WILSON LABS

Tree Frog Beer!

Harvard – Biological Labs

TOAD JUICE OR NOTHING!

HARVARD – BIOLOGICAL LABS

It's more fun to play squash than to grow it.

Cornell – Plant Sciences

My kingdom for some chapstick.

Boston U – Stone Science Building

IS THERE ANYBODY OUT THERE?

– BELOW –

NO

U MASS – GOODELL LIBRARY

I'm sorry world, I take it all back.

Amherst – Frost Library

THIS IS THE END, MY FRIEND, THE END.

SUNY ALBANY – HUMANITIES

DONE!

HARVARD – GEORGE GUND HALL

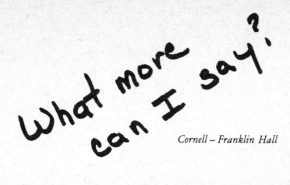

Cornell – Franklin Hall

If you have been able to find the mysteries of success in the graffiti of the Northeast's students, we applaud you. On the other hand, if you find that some of the mystery remains, then perhaps we can be of further assistance.

While traveling about the Northeastern colleges, we discovered certain characteristics that distinguished them from similar institutions in other areas of the country. Perhaps these differences are helpful in unraveling the puzzle of Northeastern dominance.

First of all there is, of course, the ivy. That may be the answer, but it is doubtful, since some campuses, including some Ivy League campuses, have virtually no ivy.

There is more granite in the Northeast, perhaps a molder of character.

The Northeast has more snow than the South or the West Coast, but no more than the Midwest.

There are differences in bathroom architecture in the Northeast. Nowhere else does one find so much marble. Nowhere else does one find stall doors that open in the center.

Campus buildings themselves provide an intellectual challenge. It is often difficult to tell from the exterior what might be an administrative or office building, classroom or residence hall.

No other school has been found to compare with the futuristic architecture of SUNY Albany.

Few campuses in the country have mastered the art of "self-destruct" architecture as well as U Mass.

Nowhere else do buildings have so many entrances that do not interconnect on the inside (except, of course, the Inner Quad at Stanford).

145

More toilets are located in the basement in the Northeast, clearly a contributor to success.

The Northeast's schools tend to be smaller than those in other areas.

There is the clamor of major urban centers: Harvard, BU, Columbia, NYU, CCNY.

Given the serenity of Dartmouth and Cornell, there is a greater contrast in atmospheres in the Northeast.

We saw more Western-style boots at Yale than at Texas or Arizona.

We did not find disposable toilet-seat covers, as are mandatory stall fixtures in the West Coast schools.

We should not forget the preppies. Though they may be found in other areas of the country, there is little question that preppies prefer the Northeast.

More dogs run free on Northeast campuses.

Nowhere are campus denizens more aloof than at Harvard.

There are more statues of founders at Northeast campuses.

Nowhere did we find sidewalk graffiti outside the Northeast. It was especially abundant at Boston College.

Last, we would like to note one other difference that may explain the success of the Northeast. This is the driving habits experienced in some areas. So significant was this factor that Marina was moved to poetry.

The first and last time I was in Boston
I spent most of the time lost on
roads that went neither west nor east.

Signs are virtually non-existent,
or readable only by the persistent
who circle 'round the block twice at least.

Now I understand how the local purist
who, wanting to deflect tourists,
has removed all directions from sight.

So it's not that the drivers are war-like.
But all left turns put you on the Mass Pike.
The State Motto must be "Bear to the right!"

Marina N. Haan
Richard B. Hammerstrom

KNOCK YOUR SOCKS OFF!!!
See what other campuses are up to from the *inside*!!

SHARE YOUR FAVORITE GRAFFITI WITH US.

No purchase is necessary to qualify. Simply send in your favorite pieces of graffiti on a 3 x 5 index card along with the source of your pieces (for example, campus building and name of school). If they are used in forthcoming sequels of our graffiti books, you will be notified and sent a free copy of our next great book.

> Send to: **Reader's Favorite Graffiti**
> **Brown House Galleries**
> **P. O. Box 4243**
> **Madison, WI 53711**

Submission of favorite graffiti by readers constitutes your permission for accepted graffiti to be published in any sequels.

—MARINA N. HAAN
—RICHARD B. HAMMERSTROM